DISCUSSION PAPER 41

The Dynamics of Post-Conflict Reconstruction and Peace Building in West Africa

Between Change and Stability

OLAWALE ISMAIL

NORDISKA AFRIKAINSTITUTET, UPPSALA 2008

Indexing terms
Conflicts
Peacebuilding
Peacekeeping
Post-conflict reconstruction
Peace agreements
Regional organizations
Economic Community
of West African States ECOMOG
West Africa
Liberia
Sierra Leone

*The opinions expressed in this volume are those of the author
and do not necessarily reflect the views of Nordiska Afrikainstitutet.*

Language checking: Elaine Almén
ISSN 1104-8417
ISBN 978-91-7106-637-4
© the author and Nordiska Afrikainstitutet 2008

Contents

Abstract 4

Foreword 5

Introduction 6

Evolution of the Global Peace Building Regime 10

Observations on Contemporary Peace Building 14

The Architecture of Peace Building in West Africa 24

Back to Praxis: The Un-making of Peace Building in Sierra Leone 32

Conclusion 40

Bibliography 42

Abstract

This essay problematizes the phenomenon of peace building, especially in post-conflict settings in West Africa. It raises questions on the conception, logic, origin, ideology and practice of post-conflict peace building. In addition, it explores the extent to which the extant peace building project could and does achieve negative peace (cessation of direct and physical violence) and positive peace (the transformation of the inherent conflictual relationships, structures, practices and interactions in society). It argues that extant peace building in West Africa is wrongly embedded in peacekeeping (as opposed to vice versa); that current practices are geared towards negative, rather than positive peace; that external (extra-African) actors determine the strategic objectives and directions; and that current peace building primarily reflects the global (international) priorities of third parties (Western countries), with local priorities being a lesser consideration. Finally, it concludes that extant logic and practice of peace building is programmed to achieve stability (especially at the macro, regime level) rather than change, and "security" rather than "peace".

Key Words: Conflict, Peace building, Peacekeeping, Post-Conflict Reconstruction, Peace Agreement, ECOWAS, ECOMOG, Sierra Leone, Liberia, West Africa and Liberal Peace.

Foreword

This discussion paper explores the ramifications of a United Nations and donor-community supported agenda of post-conflict reconstruction and peace building in West Africa. Drawing on a post-conflict state, Sierra Leone, where the UN (and the Economic Community of West African States – ECOWAS) has been deeply involved in elaborate postwar reconstruction and peace building programmes, the author provides much needed 'snapshots' of the nature and impact of international peace building on post-conflict West Africa.

The Dynamics of Post-Conflict Reconstruction and Peace Building in WestAfrica: Between Change and Stability provides information that will animate much discussion and debate on the nature and impact of internationally driven peace building agendas on African post-conflict settings. It also provides a critique of the dominant liberal peace paradigm that underpins international peace building through an up-to-date evaluation of the ways it has contributed to a misdiagnosis of the challenge of postwar peace in the West African sub-region, and how the practice of peace building has largely failed to address the roots of war and, paradoxically, fed into a near-return to the pre-conflict situation.

By focusing on the history of peace building in general and the ways in which West African States – through ECOWAS – have tapped into the global discourse of peace building, and by appropriating it into its peacekeeping processes and institutions, the paper provides an additional and much-needed critique of ECOWAS's peace building agenda. As such, this discussion paper addresses one of the core themes of the NAI Post-Conflict Transition programme, as its focus and content strike at the heart of the war-to-peace transition problematic in Africa. The discussion paper is expected to be relevant to the interests and concerns of scholars, policy makers, media practitioners and members of the public keen on a deeper understanding of the full ramifications of the challenge of sustainable peace in Africa.

Cyril I. Obi
Programme Coordinator
Post-Conflict Transition, the State and Civil Society in Africa
The Nordic Africa Institute, Uppsala, Sweden.

Introduction

This paper explores the post-conflict reconstruction and peace building problematic in West Africa. It critically examines the nature, purpose, design and ideological foundations of various attempts to rebuild post-conflict states and consolidate peace in West Africa (Paris 2004:32). The challenges of peace building are critically analyzed. They include the embedding of peace under different layers of the peacekeeping and peace building processes, involving multiple actors, unclear entry and exit points, and including the inherent contradictions and tensions in the liberal peace paradigm. Peace building means different things to varied actors and observers. The focus of this essay is on post-conflict peace building in societies emerging from internecine civil wars that approximate Kaldor's (2001) "new wars"[1] thesis. The United Nations definition of peace building as an "action to identify and support structures which will tend to strengthen and solidify peace in order to avoid a relapse into conflict"[2] is adopted within the context of this paper. This is also taken as a point of departure for interrogating post-conflict reconstruction and peace building with a view to assessing the sustainability of the contemporary "normalization" regime. In this regard, questions are raised about the possibilities of extant peace-building as a derivative of Cox's "riot control"?:[3] To what extent do contemporary intervention strategies serve to relocate violence from the public to private spheres, and thereby achieve strategic, state and regime stability, as opposed to the transformation of societies? How do current interventions approximate prophylactic strategies designed to serve the strategic objective of interveners – that is to police the socioeconomic, political, cultural and security frontiers of a real and imaginary liberal zone of peace and empire of liberty (Berger 2006:8, Duffield 2001)? And to what extent do extant interventions essentialize peace building, thus constituting a "regime of truth"?[4]

Admittedly, postwar reconstruction and peace building predates 1990 and transcends West Africa on account of the post-1945 Marshall Plan in Western Europe and the expanded mandates of UN peacekeeping missions in Namibia and Cambodia. Paris (2004:1), for instance, notes that civil wars accounted for 94% of all armed conflicts in the world in the 1990s and that between 1989 and 1999 at least 14 peace building missions were launched to consolidate peace in Angola, Mozambique, Rwanda, Cambodia, Bosnia, Croatia, Guatemala and El Salvador, among others. Also, the United Nations has launched over 55 peace operations since 1945, of which over 80% began after 1989 and at least 30% have been under way since 2003 (Dobbins 2003:88). The analyses of multiple experiments at

---

1. See subsequent sections for my description of Kaldor's new war thesis.
2. This definition is contained in the 1992 UN Secretary General's Report 'An Agenda for Peace', (June 1992:para 5).
3. Cox cited in Pugh (2004:41).
4. This is from Foucauldian thought. Practice here relates to "… places where what is said and what is done, rules imposed and reasons given, the planned and the taken for granted meet and interconnect. To analyze 'regimes of practices' means to analyze programmes of conduct which have both prescriptive effects regarding what is to be done (effects of 'jurisdiction'), and codifying effects regarding what is to be known (effects of 'veridiction')" (Foucault 1991:75).

postwar reconstruction and peace building reveal frequent failures or mixed results at best.[5] Krause and Jutersonke (2005:448) for example, conclude that "not only do about half of all peace support operations (including both peacekeeping and more expansive peace building operations) fail after around five years, but there also seems to be no clear idea of what 'success' or 'failure' actually means, nor of what an appropriate timeframe for measuring success might be". If the poor success rate of pre-2000 peace building was generally seen as being rooted in, or as purely administrative and technical matters, post-2001 global dynamics have heightened the politicization and ultimately the securitization of peace building. The post-2001 American-led War on Terror and major revisions of the global geo-strategic security calculus have made post-conflict reconstruction, peace building and state-building not only buzz-words, but key drivers of foreign policy in Western capitals. Thus Kosovo, Afghanistan and Iraq assumed prominence in this respect because of prioritized geopolitical and strategic linkages to the socioeconomic well-being and security of major global powers.

West Africa is also a major location for post-conflict reconstruction and peace building. This derives from the sub-region's appalling record of insecurity, civil war and state collapse since the 1990s, not least in Liberia, Sierra Leone, Côte d'Ivoire, Niger and Guinea-Bissau. Indeed, the sub-region significantly epitomized the widespread deterioration in security across Africa in the 1990s. The Stockholm International Peace Research Institute (SIPRI 2002:65) notes the continent's unenviable record of 19 of the total of 57 armed conflicts across the globe between 1990 and 2001. The civil wars of the 1990s and their "legacy" of recurring insecurity have sharply demonstrated the umbilical linkages between security and development. The challenges of conflict prevention, peace building and development encapsulated in Duffield's "Global Liberal Order" (2001:2) is most acute, not only in individual countries, but also assumes a sub-regional dimension in West Africa.

In interrogating peace building in West Africa, the extent to which post-conflict reconstruction, alongside violent conflicts and government dysfunctionalities, reshape the boundaries, powers, functions, size and domineering roles of the state in agenda setting, is explored. In this regard, the proper sphere of intervention (is it rebuilding institutions and society?); the interests driving interventions and interveners relative to place and time; and the scientificity of different forms of interventions (convictions about how it guarantees peace and security) are interrogated. Also, the extent to which extant peace building attempts to "re-governmentalize"[6] the state – that is, reinvent the state – and how this is informed by or informs previous experiences at state building in Africa is critically analyzed. Does it become Young's

---

5. For an evaluation of the record of peace building, see Dobbins et al. (2007), Paris (2004), Duffield (2001, 2007), Krause and Jutersonke (2005).

6. This comes from Foucault's idea of govermentality (the rationality of government). It is also about the "ensemble formed by the institutions, procedures, analyses and reflections, the calculations and tactics that allow the exercise of this very specific, albeit complex form of power, which has as its target population, as its principal form of knowledge political economy, and as its essential technical means apparatus of security" (Foucault 1991:102).

(2004)[7] possible experiment and transition into a "post-post" or "neo-post" colonial state in Africa? The problematization of extant conflicts and post-conflict peace building exposes and illuminates several interesting and important paradoxes: for instance, between stability and change; peace and security; reform and transformation; imposition of liberal peace and Fukuyama's (2005:XV) "light-footprint" (short term and minimal cost of engagement); and between mere reconstruction or rebuilding and invention. Similarly, post-conflict settings underline the paradox between the need for a big and a small state; set time-lines and endless engagement (dependency); and between humanitarianism and political realism, or militant humanitarianism.

The key objective is to re-examine post-conflict peace building as formulated and practised as a viable and only regime of truth with a view to stimulating recognition of the need for and building of alternative regimes of truths and a variety of "liberal peaces" (Cooper 2005:464). This comes from a belief that an uncritical and poor conceptual basis of post-conflict peace building can be problematic because of the kinds of goals and objectives being formulated; the unsustainability of its policies, institutions and structures over the long term; and the impact on populations beyond power elites and warlords. This essay relies heavily on secondary sources, including published academic journals and books, media reports and previous and ongoing research on conflict and security in West Africa.

The conception and practice of contemporary post-conflict peace building in West Africa is tailored to stability rather than change, and "security" as opposed to "peace". Inherent in this assertion is the debate about the possibility or impossibility of achieving change and stability and peace and security simultaneously. It is contended that external actors, faced with the highly conflictual, costly and time-consuming nature of change processes (Pearce 2005:47), discreetly and rationally opt for stability and security as opposed to transformation in post-conflict societies in West Africa and other Third World countries. The stability-security goals are limited to regimes (state-level), coated in a liberal orthodoxy and designed to achieve the political and geo-strategic objectives of interveners, including protecting the statist international system, stemming refugee outflows and undercutting potential infrastructures of transnational terrorism.

The foregoing view is founded on three interrelated subtexts: first is the reality that extant post-conflict peace building is often reduced to, or synonymous with peacekeeping and post-conflict reconstruction (defined as the physical rebuilding and/or reform of socioeconomic, political and security institutions and capacities after peace accords) (Williams 2005:6; Dobbins et al. 2007:XXXVI; Fukuyama 2006:7; Kaldor 2001:133). Peacekeeping and post-conflict reconstruction as components and phases in the peace building continuum overlap with, but do not equate with

---

7. Crawford Young (2004) argues that qualitative changes in the level and degree of stateness in Africa warrant significant changes in and departures from the current description of African states as post-colonial entities. It is from this that I propose the possibility of "post-post" or "neo-post" colonial statehood. For details, see Young (2004).

peace building. As such, the transformative goal of peace building involves, but transcends the rituals of cleansing, right sizing (down sizing) or invention of bureaucracies (Montgomery and Rondinelli 2004:27). It is the view in this essay that traditional and expanded peacekeeping (Peace Support Operations – PSO)[8] and institutional re-engineering represent only technical and administrative tasks designed to prevent a relapse into Galtung's "direct violence". Meanwhile, the more enduring and demanding peace building centred on transforming inherent "structural violence" and achieving "positive peace" are either downplayed or considered insignificant relative to regime stability, at least in the short term. The failure of the sub-region's main security actor and apparatus – the Economic Community of West African States (ECOWAS) – to articulate any policy or institutional mechanisms for peace building beyond peacekeeping or at best, peace-support operations, tangentially illustrates this.

Second, the emphasis on a "security first approach" and a relapse into "peace-as-collusion" – paying-off of warlords and factions for peace (Keen 2008:175) – sacrifices resources and commitments towards sub-national peace building. Hence, the skewing of peace accords to co-opt and reward potential spoilers legitimises new relationships of power and relocates violence from the public (state-level) to domestic, private and community domains (Heathershaw 2007:219; Tull and Mehler 2005:376; Keen 2008:172).

Third, the overarching role and powers of external actors as drivers of peace building, underpinned by the moral and ideological commitment to liberal reforms as the ultimate source of domestic and international security, wrongly assumes war and peace as diametrical opposites (Keen 2008:211). It also attempts to securitize democracy, as opposed to democratising security, and represents a Foucaultian technology of "normalization" – part of a systematic creation, classification and control of anomalies in the constituents (states) that comes from the promise to isolate and normalise deviant behaviours (civil wars and state collapse) (Dreyfus and Rabinow 1982:195). Hence, "normality is identified with democracy; abnormality with non-democratic rule" (Zanotti 2006:151). The liberal and neo-liberal emphasis of extant peace building thus becomes a technology of intervention, control, policing, security and projection of liberal internationalism (Rubinstein 2005; Paris 2004; Duffield 2001; Duffield 2007). Even where liberal peace is a viable strategy for transforming post-conflict societies to achieve positive peace (Guttal 2005), key questions arise over its implementation, especially in relation to the sequencing and pacing of reforms and institutionalization (Paris 2004).

The rest of this essay is divided into five parts. The first two sections address the evolution and limitations of contemporary peace building. They underline the theoretical and practical elasticity of peace building, as much as the limits of its liberal ideological foundations. The third section examines the role and place of West Af-

---

8. Peace support operations cover the broad spectrum of activities, including peace enforcement, designed to secure physical security and launch war-shattered societies on to long term recovery and transformation. For example, see Curran and Woodhouse (2007) and Stedman, Rothschild and Cousens (2002).

rica in the emergent peace building discourse and architecture in the post-cold war period. Attention is also focused on the limited conceptual understanding and practices of peace building, especially its uncritical conflation and confusion with peacekeeping and post-conflict reconstruction. As such, the section showcases peace building in war-torn states in the sub-region, including those undertaken by ECOWAS, as reflecting international (mis)understanding, in addition to serving the geo-strategic objective of regime stability and security of developed countries. The fourth section examines the practice and reality of peace building in Sierra Leone. This provides a case to underscore the claims about the scant and inconsequential commitment and attention to the lower end, but crucial components of peace building in West Africa. It is, however, important to note that while the limited value of passing a definitive judgment on the outcome of peace building in a rather fluid ten-year period is acknowledged, such judgment nonetheless serves as an early indicator of the problems besetting the liberal peace agenda in Africa. The final section is the conclusion that summarizes preceding arguments, examines the prospects for peace and reinforces the essay's central thesis.

Evolution of the Global Peace Building Regime

In the run up to the 1990s, international relations were marked by qualitative and quantitative changes in the nature, meaning, manifestations and scale of security dynamics. Ideologically, the end of the Cold War engendered a quasi-global ideological (liberal) consensus on peace and security that translated into heightened media and diplomatic emphasis on humanitarianism. Second, the successive progress in peace negotiations in relation to ongoing decolonization and other conflicts occasioned the rapid expansion of UN's scope of peacekeeping beyond the traditional interposition of "neutral" and observational forces in buffer zones.

Thus, the peacekeeping mandates of UN missions in Namibia (1989), Angola (1991), El Salvador (1991), Cambodia (1992), Mozambique (1992) and Bosnia (1995) were expanded to include new tasks, such as organizing elections and electoral reforms, institutional reforms and rebuilding, post-conflict reconstruction, human rights protection, demilitarization and resettlement of refugees (Miall et al. 1999:195). More importantly, while a majority of the conflicts and missions listed above predated the 1990s, across the Third World newer forms and more daunting "complex emergencies" emerged that challenged the customary understandings of war, peace and security; and the local and international dichotomy. In sub-Saharan Africa (SSA), the implosion of states and the eruption of violent conflict in Liberia, Somalia, Sierra Leone, Democratic Republic of Congo (DRC), Burundi and Rwanda came to define the phenomenon of state collapse and failure.[9]

---

9. State failure is generally defined in terms of a government's or regime's inability to perform or discharge its legal functions, while collapse relates to eroded institutional capacity to carry out activities. For extensive discourse on state failure and collapse, see Chomsky (2006), Milliken (ed.) (2003), and Zartman (ed.) (1995).

The cataclysmic conflicts in these locations defined Kaldor's "new wars" because of their intrinsic capacity to blur the orthodox "… distinctions between war (usually defined as violence between states or organized political groups for political motives), organized crime (violence undertaken by privately organized groups for private purposes, usually financial gain) and large-scale violations of human rights (violence undertaken by states or politically organized groups against individuals)" (2001:2). The new wars are linked to globalization in terms of their cause and effects, founded on the loss of stateness (eroded capacity of governments to function, including maintaining Weberian monopoly of violence), and signpost the paradoxical appearance of local and global influences (in war economies and financing) and modernity (use of modern technologies, including arms and information technology) and primitiveness (civilian sufferings) (ibid: 5–12; Bojicic-Dzelilovic 2002:82–3). It is in realization of this that Fukuyama (2005: XIX), like many other scholars, concluded that:

> The end of the Cold War left a band of failed and weak states stretching from the Balkans through Caucasus, the Middle East, Central Asia, and South Asia. State collapse or weakness had already created major humanitarian and human rights disasters during the 1990s in Somalia, Haiti, Cambodia, Bosnia, Kosovo, and East Timor.

> For a while, the United States and other countries could pretend these problems were just local, but September 11 proved that state weakness constituted a huge strategic challenge as well … Suddenly the ability to shore up or create from whole cloth of missing state capabilities and institutions has risen to the top of the global agenda and seems likely to be a major condition for security in important parts of the world.

Fukuyama's submission is important for setting the scene about the phases of the discourse and evolution of contemporary peace building since 1990. This relates to the conceptual and practical (policy) transition from traditional peacekeeping to state (institutional) building and to humanitarianism. The other transition moves the discourse and practice from "sheer" humanitarianism to political realism or militant humanitarianism or the relief and reconstruction complex (Bello 2006:281), and to a technology of normalization and security for liberal peace (Duffield 2001, 2007). I strongly relate the changes in the discourse and practice – nature, meaning, manifestation, actors and structure – of peace building to the new wars and the challenges (often constructed as threats) they posed to global humanitarian, moral, political (liberal), economic and security consensus and regimes (stability).

Yet, the advent of an asymmetrical agenda of peace building in the global conceptual and policy agenda hardly precluded contestations about its meaning, strategies and, lately, its ideological underpinnings. To foreground these contestations, Keen (2000:14), in seeking to problematize the phenomenon of War and Peace, raised the crucial observation that "we hear about rehabilitation, reconstruction, resettlement and all the various 're's' of post-conflict work. But if you could recreate and reconstruct the exact social and economic conditions prevailing at the outset of a civil war, would it simply break out all over again – for the same reasons as before?" From this perspective, questions arise such as: What is peace building? What are its components, phases, markers, tasks and objectives? Who can undertake peace building? And what are the ideological and geopolitical undercurrents of peace building?

The intellectual foundation of contemporary peace building appears to be rooted in peace research and conflict-resolution literature and the writings of peace theorists. According to Miall et al. (1999:36), peace building refers to "the attempt to overcome the structural, relational and cultural contradictions which lie at the root of conflict". While it is acknowledged that actions, including diplomatic negotiations such as shuttle and two-track diplomacies, are historical phenomena and elements of broader peace building, the conceptual foundation of contemporary peace building is often related to Galtung's tripartite approaches to peace – peacekeeping, peacemaking and peace building. Miall et al. (1999:186–7) reproduced aspects of Galtung's (1975) thesis that defined peacekeeping as actions seeking "to halt and reduce the manifest violence of the conflict through the intervention of military forces in an interpository role"; peacemaking as actions that are "directed at reconciling political and strategic attitudes through mediation, negotiation, arbitration and conciliation mainly at the elite level"; and peace building as actions and propositions that addressed "the practical implementation of peaceful social change through socioeconomic reconstruction and development".

Other peace theorists reinforce this narrative by linking contemporary peace building to the distinction between structural and direct violence, and between negative and positive peace. Galtung (1964:95) in his *Structural Theory of Aggression*, links violence to "drives towards change, even against the will of others". Structural violence is linked to practices embedded in relationships that marginalize, impoverish and disempower people, and cause a crisis of "rising expectations" that produces frustration and aggression (Gurr 1970:9–13; Runciman 1966:9). Direct violence relates to physical attacks, injuries, threats, harassment and intimidation. Peace, often uncritically assumed as the flipside of violence, in Galtung's tradition is assumed to be negative when marked by cessation of only direct violence, and positive when it transforms society by achieving an ideal social justice, removes structural violence and allows people to flourish and live their full lifespan (Fetherston 2000:202; Mani 2005:28).

The missing relational dimension of peace building in Galtung's formulation was included in Lederach's Conflict Transformation approach to peace building that emphasized the transformative goal of peace building. This sees peace building as transcending the resolution of specific problems to focus on the content, context and structure of relationships. Hence, "conflict transformation envisions and responds to the ebb and flow of social conflict as life-giving opportunities for creating constructive change processes that reduce violence, increase justice to direct interaction and social structures, and respond to real-life problems in human relationships" (2003: 14). Through this, peace theorists identify reducing the relapse into direct violence and contributing to conditions for socioeconomic and political recovery and reconciliation as the primary goals, and the transformation of relationships and society as the ultimate goal of peace building (Ramsbotham 2000:172; Miall et al. 1999:60).

The evolution of peace building is linked to the 1992 UN Secretary General (Boutros Boutros-Ghali) Report – *An Agenda for Peace* – where peace building was explicitly defined as "action to identify and support structures which will tend to strengthen and solidify peace in order to avoid a relapse into conflict". The 1995 report highlighted important linkages between peace building and development and made distinctions between peacekeeping, peacemaking and peace building along the lines of Galtung's original formulation. Given the upsurge in new wars and associated humanitarian, political and socioeconomic challenges to restoring order and peace, the United Nations institutional focus, emphasis and practice has been restricted to "post-settlement" peace building. Post-settlement, a neologism for post-conflict, relates to periods and peace building actions undertaken following the signing or sometimes imposition of peace accords, terms and conditions (Miall et al. 1999:188; Borer 2006:5–7; McEvoy Levy 2006:7).

According to the UN, post-conflict peace building covers "the various concurrent and integrated actions undertaken at the end of a conflict to consolidate peace and prevent a recurrence of armed confrontation".[10] To underscore the evolutionary transitions in the policy and practice of peace building, the UN has consistently upgraded its tick-boxes of tasks included in post-accord peace building. In 1992, it included disarmament, guarding and destruction of weapons, repatriating and resettling refugees, advising and retraining security actors, monitoring elections and protection of human rights, and reforming and strengthening governmental institutions.

By 1995, in *Supplement to An Agenda for Peace and Development*, improved police and judicial systems and economic development were added, and in 1997 the provision of reintegration and rehabilitation programmes and the provision of conditions for resumed development were added.[11] By 1999, the UN peacekeeping operation manual projected multifunctionality built on flexibility of mandates and tasks to cover emergency reconstruction and positive peace building. This policy evolution translated into newer forms of peacekeeping, including second and third generation taxonomies, that emphasized the emergent focus on elections, humanitarian assistance, human rights and civilian police (Malone and Wermester 2000: 40).

The more recent UN policy conception of peace building is built upon the notion of "integrated mission", encapsulated in the 2006 "Capstone Doctrine" that combines military and civilian peacekeeping, and adds transitional administration to multifunctionality as key elements of peace building (Freeman 2007:5). Institutionally, a Peace building Commission[12]

---

10. This definition is attributed to former UN Secretary General Kofi Annan, cited in Miall et al. (1999:188).

11. For the analysis of the changing and additional tasks and elements of United Nations post-settlement peace building, see Ramsbotham (2000:176–7).

12. The Peace building Commission was created following the report and recommendation of the 2005 High-Level Panel on Threats, Challenges and Change. Its actual establishment was pursuant to Resolution 1645 of the Security Council (20 December 2005). For details, see UN 20 December 2005.

(with support offices and fund) was created in 2006 to address civilian, long term and transformative goals, initially in Sierra Leone and Burundi (Curran and Woodhouse 2007:1056; Barnett 2006:88). The commission is tasked with proposing integrated strategies for post-conflict peace building and recovery; helping to ensure predictable financing for early recovery activities and sustained financial investment over the medium- to longer-term; extending the period of attention by the international community to post-conflict recovery; and developing best practices on issues that require extensive collaboration among political, military, humanitarian and development actors.[13]

It is important to reiterate that different tasks and coverage of peace building expanded as the challenges of restoring peace and order in war-shattered states intensified in the 1990s. The integrated understanding of and approach to contemporary peace building has considerable points of comparison with state and nation building[14] (at least in American parlance). In fact, nation and state building clearly underlines contemporary peace building to be actions undertaken by outsiders and external actors. Berger (2006:6), for instance, defines it "as an externally driven, or facilitated, attempt to form or consolidate a stable, and sometimes democratic, government over an internationally recognised national territory against the backdrop of the establishment and consolidation of the UN and the universalization of a system of sovereign nation-states".[15] In spite of the impressive ascent of peace building on to the global policy agenda, the following key observations can be made.

Observations on Contemporary Peace Building

(a) It is worth reiterating that changes in the conception and policy manifestations of peace building have paralleled changes in the forms and levels of insecurity both locally and internationally, occasioned by new wars (the theatres of peace building). For instance, the nature of new wars in themselves – typified by the radical rupturing and destruction of institutions of government and unparalleled humanitarian catastrophes and human rights violations – informed the transition from traditional to second and third generation peacekeeping. Indeed, the approximation of peace building and state building signposts the extent of destruction and needed reconstruction. Similarly, the February 2000 introduction and inclusion of child protection advisors in peacekeeping missions is foregrounded by the upsurge in child soldiering.[16] The same can be said of including post-conflict socioeconomic and political reform and construction in the mandates of peacekeepers. Also, the reality of the long-term challenges of peace building, rooted in the transformation tasks and goals of peace building in war-shattered so-

---

13. For details of the commission's mandates and activities in Sierra Leone and Burundi, see http://www.un.org/peace/peace building/.
14. This represents an alternative intellectual foundation for peace building, founded exclusively on American experiences in military intervention and reconstruction efforts since World War II. For example, see Dobbins et al. (2003) and Gennip (2005).

15. Similarly, Simonsen (2004) relates it to nation building because of the dual emphasis on reconciliation and the fostering of unity and a national, less-conflictual identity. See also, Dodge (2006) and Dobbins et al. (2007).
16. For example, see http://www.un.org/children/conflict/pr/2000-02-2214.html.

cieties, informed the establishment of the Peace building Commission. The enforcement of sanctions and embargoes on trade in natural resources was arguably informed by post-September 11, 2001 international security considerations, including the War on Terror, thus pinpointing the geopolitical and geostrategic undercurrents of peace building in Third World countries. The fact that terrorists and terror cells have been cited in illegal trade in Collier's "lootable resources",[17] including diamonds, timber, narcotics, etc, underlines this.

(b) The second observation relates to the continued conceptual limitations of peace building, in spite of the seeming consensus on its inevitability, desirability and importance. This is often expressed in the equation and interchangeable usage of peace building with development, conflict prevention, poverty alleviation, reconstruction, preventive diplomacy, etc. At one level, peacekeepers and peacekeeping have become neologisms and buzzwords for peace builders and peace building respectively. At another level, peacekeeping is separated from peace building to emphasize the latter's demilitarized, civilian nature and its foundation in social work. There is near unanimity on this. According to Hazen (2007:324), "peace building has remained a largely amorphous concept without clear guidelines or gaols. International interventions in post-conflict countries exhibited few clear examples of success, leading to pessimism about the prospects for successful peace building. The lack of agreement on the definition of peace building, what it entailed, and what it should achieve meant a lack of coordination and focus". Also, Williams (2005:546), in his historical analysis of peace building before 1945, concludes that reconstruction, a term often used interchangeably with (but more appropriately as a component of) peace building was and is "often used without any clear concept of what is meant. It is a new addition to post-war vocabulary and like many new things it is used indiscriminately and vaguely thought to mean everything that helps the return to the good old days when all were prosperous before the war".

This conceptual ambivalence may not be unrelated to the complicated nature of peace building itself, in which the "transition from war to peace is a complex process involving making a country safe and secure, protecting the population, reintegrating displaced population and refugees, rebuilding infrastructures, re-launching the economy, promoting good governance, establishing political dialogue and restoring social capital" (*The Courier* 2003:8). In fact, certain tasks designed to reduce direct violence may and often do jeopardize the chances and prospects of positive peace. I argue that the conceptual convolution in peace building emerges from extant practices that conceive peace building only in terms of post-settlement activities, as well as the uncritical reductionism to technical or administrative details[18] and rebuilding of

---

17. Collier relates lootable resources to the primary products included in a country's export earnings and which can be exploited for profit-making opportunities by combatants and warring factions in armed conflict. For details, see Collier (2000).

18. Most of the literature emphasizing technical details and dimensions of peace building is associated with America's experience in nation and state building. For instance, Dobbins et al. (2007) provide details of police and peacekeepers to civilian ratios in peace building, while Williams (2005) focuses on key infrastructures and their rebuilding in peace building.

institutions and infrastructures (post-conflict reconstruction). For a start, the restriction of peace building to the post-conflict or post-settlement period presents its own ambiguities, as the term "post" is problematic and can often be a misnomer, given the possibility of violence beyond the signing of peace accords or its relocation to other sub-national levels.

Importantly, the transformative goal of peace building incorporates elements of negative and positive peace, as the cessation of direct violence often paves the way for transforming structural violence. As such, peace building conceptually can neither be restricted to post-accord activities nor separated from peacekeeping (as is sometimes suggested).[19] Building on extant works,[20] like Ryan (2000:34) who proposes five stages of conflict and, by inference, peace building (pre-violence, escalation, endurance, de-escalation and post-violence), it is possible to identify three possible functional typologies of peace building (pre-conflict, wartime and post-conflict), founded on the timing of intervention and activities along the conflict continuum. Pre-conflict peace building emphasizes traditional preventive diplomacy, involving negotiations, trade-offs and compromises designed to resolve differences amicably without resorting to violence. Wartime peace building covers Galtung's peacemaking, including initiatives undertaken in the heat of battle to first secure cessation of hostilities (direct violence) and lay the foundation for further ceasefires and negotiations. Post-conflict peace building covers activities undertaken after obligatory and/or imposed peace terms.

The functional classification hardly precludes connections between the three typologies, for all belong to the same conflict continuum. To be sure, Ryan (2000:39) contends that "separating peacekeeping and peace building has become difficult because 'second generation' missions perform peace building tasks but under the title of peacekeeping. There is very little in the literature on the peacekeeping dimensions of peace building, yet there is a clear overlap between the two approaches". Following from the extant works of Last (2000) and Duffield (2001), the key tasks of peace building are identified as including the restoration of security, governance, development activities, provision of humanitarian relief and promoting reconciliation. In this regard, at least five components of post-settlement peace building (since it is the focus of this essay and predominates in global policy) through which these tasks can be achieved are identified. The first is disarmament, demobilization and reintegration (DDR) of combatants to demilitarize society and curb the de-monopolization of violence by government (Berdal 1996). The second is post-conflict reconstruction that emphasizes the rebuilding of physical infrastructure in socioeconomic, political and secu-

---

19. For example, Hazen (2007) and a majority of peace research and conflict resolution literature make this claim.
20. Similarly, Wentges (1998:59) proposed four functional dimensions (preventive, reduction/alleviation, containment and settlement). Also, Etzioni (2004) proposes three core elements of nation-building (peace building, including forging new national identity; good governance; and economic development). Natsios (2005) also proposes nine principles of post-conflict reconstruction and development, including ownership, capacity building, sustainability, selectivity, results, partnerships, flexibility, accountability and assessment.

rity spheres. It also involves the reconstitution of the state (regimes and governance) and multiple and simultaneous reforms of politics, economics, state-societal (social and civil society) relations, justice systems and the security sector (Addison 2003 &1998; Addison and Murshed 2001).

The third is reconciliation, defined as the transformation of relationships at various levels of society through negotiation and justice (restitutive and reparative) in the form of amnesties, trials, truth commissions and human rights commissions (Blagojevic 2007:555). The fourth component is humanitarian provisioning, which emphasizes the broad range of emergency services and assistance to people in theatres of peace building, including the protection and resettlement of refugees and internally displaced persons and emergency food aid.

The final component is social re-engineering that projects the long-term goal of transforming conflictual relationships, reduces violent dissensus and seeks to evolve or transform identities. Again, the intense oscillation, overlaps and interconnectedness between these components are emphasized, thereby foreclosing any mutual exclusivity. This conceptual clarification is especially important given the tendency, especially in some extant literature (peace research), to exclude peacekeeping and even pre-conflict interventions from peace building, and the separation of actors and practitioners (Richmond 2004:84). As such, the integrated notion of peace building comes from the reality that to build peace requires different elements, resources and capacities, and is ultimately sustainable if it embraces the principles of prevention (Schnabel 2002:7). Admittedly, this essay does not pretend to resolve the conceptual impasse in the larger peace building literature: however, it provides some conceptual clarifications and brings out the contradictions in the liberal peace paradigm and practice in clear relief.

(c) Extant peace building is skewed towards alleviating direct violence, and is also preoccupied with stability rather than change and with security as opposed to peace. This argument is founded on the tendency to see and practise peace building as securing or imposing peace treaties (through a power-sharing model), undertaking DDR and elections, reconstructing the limited infrastructure central to a regime's domestic stability, as well as preserving (reintegrating) the state's external status. Apart from the limited conception and practice to include the lower end (long term engagement to promote change and transformation – structural violence) of peace building, the study draws attention to some limitations of peace accords, DDR and post-conflict reconstruction. The criticisms relate to their individual and collective incapacity to promote long-term change and security at the sub-national level. Regarding the nature of peace agreements, it is observed that a majority, especially in SSA, are explicitly or implicitly guided by a power-sharing model that shares (rewards) the spoils of war and peace among factional elites/warlords and excludes other stakeholders,[21] thereby imposing "perpetrators' justice". Tull and Mehler (2005:376), focusing on post-Cold War peace processes in Africa, especially in the DRC (Lusaka Accord), Liberia (all

---

21. For instance, Sorensen (1998) notes how peace agreements exclude women and their concerns and priorities in post-conflict planning and peace building.

peace treaties signed since the 1990s, including the 2003 Comprehensive Peace Agreement) and Sierra Leone (1999 Lome Accord), observed that:

> Power-sharing agreements between embattled incumbents and insurgents have emerged as the West's preferred instrument of peace-making in Africa. In almost every country in which insurgent leaders mustered sufficient military power to attract the attention of foreign states, they were included in 'governments of national unity' ... the institutionalization of this practice demonstrates Western willingness to provide political pay-offs for insurgent violence and thereby creates incentive structures which turn the rebel path into an appealing option in the pursuit of otherwise blocked political aspirations.

In the case of Sierra Leone and Liberia, the sharing of power among factions contributed to the protraction of conflicts as groups splintered and were emboldened to exploit the West's desperation for cease-fires, thereby introducing and intensifying the "gaming of violence" element in peace building.[22] From this, Tull and Mehler (2005:377) conclude that "... the West's preferred instrument of conflict resolution – power-sharing agreements – turns the rhetoric of conflict prevention on its head in that it inadvertently encourages would-be leaders elsewhere to embark on the insurgency path". To underscore the West's widespread usage of this "security first" approach, Goodhand and Sedra (2007), in their analysis of the post-conflict reconstruction regime in Afghanistan, argue that the 2001 Bonn Agreement and the subsequent inflow of aid represented a package of bribes for security as they undercut known, logical principles of using aid conditionalities for peace consolidation. The premising of post-conflict peace building on a "faulty" security-at-all-costs platform could and often endangers post-settlement peace building, as was the case in Liberia during the 1996–97 Peace Process that transformed Charles Taylor from a rebel warlord into president. The institutionalization of power sharing thus exacerbates the inherent tension between activities undertaken to achieve negative and positive peace.

The current understanding and planning of the DDR component is also criticized for being poorly conceived as a set of technical activities (weapons collection, storage and destruction) with few if any strategic linkages to the consolidation of democracy and isolated from the intensely political and politicized peace building processes. According to Berdal (1996:5–6), DDR can be conceptualized:

> ... as a set of distinct activities that require advance planning and outside assistance, these are all intensely political processes whose long-term and sustainable impact depend on parallel efforts of political and economic reconstruction to resolve, or ameliorate as far as possible, the root causes of conflict. Disarmament, demobilization and reintegration cannot, in other words, be treated simply as a set of managerial or administrative challenges, as a number of institutions, non-governmental organizations (NGOs) and donors have been prone to do.

This assertion played-out quite well in Liberia during the 1996-97 peace building process where scant attention, in the form of a lack of external (Western) support for

---

22. Also, on the splintering effect of power-sharing peace agreements, see Darby (2006:6).

ECOWAS's Ceasefire Monitoring Group's (ECOMOG) continued post-settlement (post-election) disarmament, demobilization and reintegration programmes, allowed Charles Taylor to manipulate the process, expel ECOMOG and prepare the country for the subsequent resumption of violent insurgencies (Olonisakin 2000; Aboagye 1999). Berdal's conclusion appears still relevant, almost a decade afterwards. McMullin (2004:626) in his analysis of DDR processes in Mozambique (an oft-cited success story of peace building) noted that Mozambique's demobilization and reintegration programmes (DRPs) were conceived and undertaken with the sole objective of avoiding a worst-case scenario (full-blown civil war). Therefore, they failed to address broader, long-term threats, including ex-combatants' entrenched involvement in and control of organized criminal networks (drugs and arms). They also lacked adequate factoring of politics into the process to the extent that unforeseen fall-outs of the DRPs have fuelled political mistrust and dissensus that impact negatively on Mozambique's postwar peace and development progress. The same conditions appear to characterize the process in Sierra Leone (as will be seen in subsequent sections) in which DDR is largely geared towards preventing challenges to regime stability and security, and securing a "quick-exit" for external (Western) interveners.

The post-conflict reconstruction component is undoubtedly the lynchpin of the current conception and practice of peace building. In general, it is "the rebuilding of the socio-economic framework of society and the reconstruction of the enabling conditions for a functioning peacetime society [to include] the framework of governance and the rule of law".[23] As noted earlier, it involves reforms to the political, economic, security and judicial (justice) sectors. Political reconstruction involves the review or designing of new constitutions, holding of elections to create the legal basis for domestic and international legitimacy for regimes, and founding or resuscitating supporting institutions (parliament, political parties, civil society and pressure groups, etc).

A critical element in political reconstruction is democratization – suggesting peace building as democracy building (Plattner 2005). This includes the (re)construction of a raft of political institutions, rules and activism tailored in terms of Western, neo-liberal values. Critically, post-conflict political reforms are now laden with attempts to further delimit the state (government) by rolling-back the scope, scale and participation of governments in the economy and to stimulate the emergence of a strong civil society to counterbalance and "police" the state. Most post-conflict political reconstruction is based on a reshaping of state-society relations through a reversal of roles and powers along the liberal state-strong society model.

The economic reconstruction component involves attempts to modernize and stimulate private sector-led economic growth by restructuring public (macroeconomic) finance through fiscal and budgetary policies (spending ceilings), monetary and inflation targets, regulation of foreign exchange, savings, investments and trade

---

23. This definition is credited to the World Bank (1998), cited in Hamre and Sullivan (2002:89). For more details on the unit's activities and mandates, see World Bank (1998:36–9) and http://www.worldbank.org/html/extdr/spring99/pcr-pb.htm.

policy (Carbonnier 1998:21–32). Also, the socioeconomic reforms are underlined by liberal values of free trade, unfettered market competition (marketization) and redefined (limited) levels of state participation (beyond regulation) in economic processes. The issues and reforms covered often represent explicit conditionalities for external financial assistance, including debt-forgiveness, funding for infrastructural rebuilding, institutional capacity building and sometimes Foreign Direct Investment (FDI).

Security Sector Reform (SSR) generally involves military re-professionalization through structural and normative reorientation (redefinition of security and the institutionalization of democratic ethos designed to enhance civilian oversight of security actors – democratizing security) (Williams 2000:2–3). In post-conflict reconstruction, Brzoka (2006:3) identifies three key elements of SSR to include DDR; the creation of new security sector institutions and the prevention of the re-emergence of repressive state security institutions apt to intervene in politics, economy and society; and building accountable, efficient and effective security forces.

The judicial and justice reform component involves rebuilding the physical infrastructure and processes of justice dispensation, usually spearheaded by third party countries through their development agencies. It also involves the implementation of transnational justice processes through the establishment of international criminal courts and war crimes tribunals to prosecute alleged wartime human rights violations. In some post-conflict contexts, the emphasis is on Truth and Reconciliation Commissions (TRCs) rather than the prosecution of war criminals. Human rights groups and non-governmental organizations, especially members of the international community, provide support and credibility to the processes of transnational justice.

In spite of the impressive array of goals associated with post-conflict reconstruction, it suffers from some conceptual and practical shortcomings. In the first instance, there are numerous conceptual inconsistencies in different components (sectoral reforms), which may be poorly coordinated, or linked with little or no assessment of the impact of simultaneous reform processes. Moreover, aspects of the reforms may undercut one another – for example, how appropriate is the model of marketization, spending caps, free trade and a small state in post-conflict contexts where the state is needed to minimise or manage disagreements emerging from the allocation of socioeconomic resources?

Pearce (2005:44) notes that "neo-liberal economics do not prioritize and often contradict urgent post-conflict tasks of employment generation for ex-combatants, sustainability of subsistence agriculture for displaced and refugee peasant populations as opposed to prioritizing export-oriented agriculture, infrastructural investment in the war-torn zones where market potential is limited …" Brzoka (2006:8), in relation to SSR, also notes, "because it challenges established power relations without immediately establishing a fixed pattern of new ones, security sector reform often results in an initial political instability". Carbonnier (1998:17) also notes that economic adjustment and the shock therapy of marketization in post-conflict theatres often contradicts political trade-offs, compromises moves towards peace and impairs reconciliation. Import liberalization could easily stifle domestic entrepreneurship through importation of non-essential goods and services or expose locals to intense competition from better-resourced global players. It can actually increase inequalities by over-rewarding winners, or paradoxically, any radical redistribution of income may provoke a violent backlash from former combatants and warlords (ibid: 46-8).

Also, transnational justice activism can and often does undermine fragile peace agreements, as was the case in Liberia in June 2003 when Charles Taylor was indicted for war crimes whilst he was still being persuaded by third parties to sign a peace treaty. This underscores the internal cross-purposes and diametrical objectives among the different elements and actors in post-conflict peace building. Still, elections and linear political power distribution could constitute sources of old and new conflicts through a "winner-takes-all" approach (Reilly 2002). The Liberian 1996–7 peace process typifies this: Taylor's election victory simply shut out other groups from mainstream political participation and power.

Post-conflict reconstruction as currently conceived and practised is only intended to resurrect the institutional base of the state and guarantee the stability of the regime in power. Perhaps, it is no coincidence that post-conflict reconstruction is sometimes seen as the beginning and end of peace building, and the fulfilling of key reconstruction (reform) tasks often signals the exit of key actors in peace building – multinational forces and the retinue of international NGOs and development agencies. For example, the UN peacekeeping mission (UNAMSIL) and the postwar reconstruction complex (other actors in peace building) withdrew from Sierra Leone in less than two years after the May 2002 elections.[24] This underlines the inherent short-term perspective in extant conceptions and practices, despite research pointing to the need for at least a five-year active engagement after accords.[25]

The post-conflict reconstruction (peace building) train thus appears like a fire-brigade crew answering emergency calls (including putting out bushfires) and moving on to the next call (theatre of conflict) almost immediately. The trigger clause for exit appears to be signposted by the appearance or semblance of regime stability and security, with or without peace and transformation. Admittedly, peacekeeping missions do not approximate the totality of peace building activities, yet the strong correlation between the presence of such missions and the intensity of peace building exposes the internal illogicality of extant practice. It appears the Peace building Commission was created to fill this institutional, conceptual and practical lacuna. Yet, the commission, as observed by Curran and Woodhouse (2007:1062–64), is limited by its technical approach, inadequate expertise and capacity for non-peacekeeping peace building activities, and importantly, lack of coherent strategy that incorporates all aspects of the peace building process. Pouligny (2005:505) makes this observation in her conclusion that the pretension

---

24. For instance, the International Crisis Group (ICG, September 2003) highlights the key challenges in Sierra Leone prior to the drawing-down of UN missions. See subsequent sections on this.
25. For example, Collier (2004) and Collier and Hoeffler (2002) argue that there is a 50% change in conflict relapse in the first five to ten years of the post-conflict period.

of building states is undercut by draining their political substance:

> We may help rebuild economic and socio-political infrastructures and institutions, but they are no more than 'empty boxes', because we have given little consideration to the conceptual roots of social and political life. In other words, we quite simply forget that politics and statehood must be understood in their 'substantial' aspects, their diverse conceptions and properties, and not only in their formal appearances.

(d) The final observation relates to the domineering role of external Western actors in the strategic direction (financing, agenda-setting, timing of entry and exit, legitimization and focus) of peace building. This has been cited by a majority of extant peace research literature[26] to criticize the intellectual foundations of contemporary peace building – as explicit evidence of a "technology' of normalization and projection of liberal internationalism. This claim, however, acknowledges the participation of non-Western actors, including peacekeeping contingents, sub-regional organizations, national governments and local non-governmental organizations.[27]

According to Paris (2004:17–39), the evolution of contemporary peace building architecture coincided with reforms in major global political, economic and security institutions (along liberal orthodoxies) that constitute the strategic drivers of peace building. It is noted that post-1990 international relations occasioned a consensus on liberal reforms in political-economic and security thinking in the United Nations, the Organization for Security and Cooperation in Europe (OSCE), European Union (EU), North Atlantic Treaty Organization (NATO), Western International Development Agencies and NGOs and the Bretton Woods Financial Institutions.

It is noted that the emerging liberal consensus is transposed into peace building in Third World countries through aid and conditionalities, institutional reform (post-conflict reconstruction) benchmarks and sometimes through military action. In particular, the refocusing of the World Bank on peace building can be gleaned from its establishment of a post-conflict reconstruction unit and fund in 1997, and an increase in lending to post-conflict countries to the tune of over 20% of total lending (Bello 2006:286). This is seen as a major reaction to the exigencies of insecurity and, more importantly, as using peace building as a mission for projecting and promoting Western strategic interests and liberal values, particularly as they relate to a liberal peace (Duffield 2007; Pugh 2004:46). From the foregoing, it can be argued that the neutral, apolitical and humanitarian appearance of peace building is in reality underpinned by concrete geostrategic and ideological calculations.

---

26. For example, see Miall et al. (1999:199) for this and a comprehensive discussion of the limitations of existing UN post-settlement peace building between 1989 and 1998.
27. Hazen (2007) argues that peace building is and should be a national project undertaken by locals, as opposed to external actors. However, this argument only talks about one aspect (social re-engineering and reconciliation) of peace building and overlooks the real-life strategic workings and determinants of peace building. Hence, it is my contention that peace building is best handled by a consortium between local and international actors, and military and civilian actors. I take up this argument in subsequent sections of this essay.

The appropriateness of the liberal peace orthodoxy as currently promoted in Third World countries has also been questioned, and rightly so, especially in relation to its "impository" nature and the complicity of International Financial Institutions (IFIs) in state failure and collapse in Africa. Paris (2004) believes in the scientificity of liberal internationalism but draws attention to its pacing and timing, arguing for the institutionalization of practices before liberalization. He contends that post-conflict settings are especially vulnerable to the pathologies of liberalization (bad civil society, ethnic entrepreneurship, elections as focal points of harmful competition, saboteurs and failed transitions, and inherent dangers of economic liberalization) because of intense societal conflicts, weak conflict dampeners and ineffective political institutions in the immediate postwar period (ibid:160–175).

Coyne (2006) queries the scant attention to the informal ("art of association") elements of socioeconomic and political liberalization. Zanotti (2006:162) reinforces the criticism of liberal peace obsession with building institutions, noting that "by singling out institutional reform as the key to bringing about 'democracy' and promoting historically situated techniques of government as universally effective, the UN has fallen short of considering how these techniques interact with local multiple formal and informal arrangements, political cultures, resources and economic situations". She concludes that "in the post-Cold War peace, democracy and development are problematized in ways that privilege institutional reforms, codification, discipline and regulatory and performance-assessment mechanisms as the key elements for social changes and as instruments for fostering international security" (ibid).

Attention is also drawn to the culpability of neo-liberal policies (structural adjustment policies in the 1980s and 1990s) and vectors (institutions – World Bank and International Monetary Fund) in the multiple cases of state failure and collapse in Africa and the dangers of relapse into conflict by intensifying radical liberal reforms in post-conflict reconstruction (Williams 2004). Keen (2008:171) notes that the imposition of liberal peace without a proper understanding of the hidden functions of war and peace undermines long-term peace and the huge potential for social changes occasioned by wartime mobilization. Bellamy (2004:29) also posits that "it is the very policies of Western states and financial institutions such as the World Bank and IMF that exacerbate the grinding poverty and patrimonial politics that are often identified as structural causes of protracted violence". He likens peace building to a "… humanitarian economy, supported entirely from abroad, based on handouts, in which nobody is paid and no-one works and in which beneficiaries experience repeated humiliation". The weakening of the public sector (rolled-back state under liberalization) is said to be a deliberate policy to accommodate the humanitarian economy.

Overall, contemporary peace building appears limited by its "ad hocism", emphasis on technical and administrative details and the proliferation of international actors (military and non-military) with divergent objectives and interests and covering different sectors, but who hardly ever coordinate their activities (Krause and Jutersonke

2005:455). The externalized determinants and militarization of peace building objectives and goals also mean considerable doubts about the ability post-conflict interventions actually have to promote the long term welfare and security and representation of local populations (Schwarz 2005). It is in this context that Mani's (2005:29) observation aptly captures the reality of contemporary peace building:

> The majority of international programmes focus on the institutions and mechanics, the form and structure, of the rule of law, while evading the substantive content – the ethos – of that rule of law. They focus on resurrecting the standardized and replicable pillars of the rule of law – the judiciary, police, and prisons – rather than addressing the content of the laws upheld by them. They focus on law enforcement – as illustrated by the preoccupation with police reform – rather than fostering the rule of law and public confidence in it. They shy away from knowledge and integration of cultural and historical specificities and the needs of individual societies, and engage local populations only minimally in their programmes.

The Architecture of Peace Building in West Africa

ECOWAS in 1990 dispatched ECOMOG to Liberia for a variety of geopolitical, humanitarian and security objectives. In 1997, the sub-regional peacekeeping force was subsequently deployed to Sierra Leone (1997), Liberia (again in 2003), Guinea-Bissau (2002) and Côte d'Ivoire (2002). By the end of the 1990s, ECOWAS and ECOMOG had become the key security and peace building institution and instrument respectively. The expansion of ECOWAS from its primary economic integration objective into peace and security activities in the 1990s signposted the changed and changing security environment in the sub-region and across Africa, the convergence of development and security, and the post-Cold War trade-off between inter and intra-state civil wars. In fact, Liberia set the trail of state failure and collapse in the Mano River Basin in 1990, with spill-over effects in neighbouring Sierra Leone, Guinea and Côte d'Ivoire (Moran 2006: 20). The inception of ECOMOG and acute insecurity in the sub-region necessitated the review of ECOWAS statutes to reflect and provide a basis for acting on peace building concerns. This was manifested in its 1993 Revised Treaty and protocols on The Mechanism for Conflict Prevention, Management, Resolution, Peacekeeping and Security (1999) and on Democracy and Good Governance (2001). These constitute the key elements in the peace building regime in West Africa.

To understand the ideological, geopolitical and intellectual underpinnings of peace building in West Africa, it is important to analyze these statutes in relation to the maintenance of peace and security. The 1999 protocol on The Mechanism for Conflict Prevention, Management, Resolution, Peacekeeping and Security is the central legal, institutional and political statute for peace building in the sub-region. It marked, in part, the attempt by West African state leaders to restructure the regional peacekeeping architecture and streamline it to adjust to and reflect external (non-West African) geostrategic and ideological (liberal peace) priorities in conformity with global patterns. Hence, it was skewed towards the stability and security of regimes and negative peace as opposed to transforming society, undercutting the structural basis of violence and positive peace.

The revised ECOWAS treaty, apart from reaffirming the primacy of economic cooperation and integration for the purpose of improving the socioeconomic conditions and welfare of people in the region (Article 3), significantly recognizes the imperative of regional peace and security. The treaty's Article 58 charged member states to "to work to safeguard and consolidate relations conducive to the maintenance of peace, stability and security within the region". It emphasizes the need for cooperation and action on cross-border security, immigration, mediation and peaceful settlement of disputes, a sub-regional peacekeeping force and early warning system and good governance. The provisions of the revised treaty, the organization's experience of peacekeeping in Liberia and recurrent cases of insecurity prompted the 1999 protocol on conflict management. The protocol in its preamble recognizes three crucial foundations of peace and security, including "good governance, rule of law and sustainable development as essential for peace and conflict prevention". The convergence of development, good governance and security was also reaffirmed under Article 2a: "that economic and social development and the security of peoples and States are inextricably linked".

The key objectives of the protocol as listed under Article 3 include, among others, preventing, managing and resolving internal and inter-state conflicts; implementing relevant aspects of Article 58 of the revised treaty; strengthening cooperation in the areas of conflict prevention, peacekeeping operations, cross-border crime and international terrorism; maintaining and consolidating peace, security and stability in the sub-region; and constituting and deploying a civilian and military force to maintain or restore peace within the sub-region whenever the need arises. The mechanisms also highlight the authority of heads of states as the highest decision-making body with powers "to act on all matters concerning conflict prevention, management and resolution, peacekeeping, security, humanitarian support, peace building, control of cross-border crime, proliferation of small arms, as well as all other matters covered by the provisions of this Mechanism" (Article 6 of 1999 Protocol).

Also, Chapter III of the protocol lists the principal organs (Defence and Security Commission, Council of Elders and ECOMOG) as key instruments of peace building in the sub-region. The Defence and Security Commission was to be composed of military and security chiefs from member states, who were charged with formulating the mandate, terms of reference and engagement, appointing force commanders and determining the composition of ECOMOG. The Council of Elders represent a tool for peaceful mediation and intervention in conflict situations. It is a collection of eminent persons from various segments of society – women, political, traditional, customary and religious leaders – who, on behalf of ECOWAS, can use their good offices and experience to play the role of mediators, conciliators and facilitators. ECOMOG, under Article 22, was recognized as the sub-region's intervention force and comprises civilian and military elements (of one battalion from each member state to make up 15 battalions) with responsibilities for observing and monitoring, peacekeeping and restoration of peace, humanitarian and disaster relief, enforcement action (embargoes and sanctions), preventive deployment, policing activities and crucially, peace building, disarmament and demobilization. Chapter V of the protocol underlines its applicability to inter-state and internal conflicts that threaten humanitarian disaster and constitutes a serious threat to peace and security in the sub-region.

Finally, Chapter IX specifically deals with peace building. Article 42 underlines the commitment of the organization to providing assistance to countries just emerging from conflict "to increase their capacity for national, social, economic and cultural reconstruction". ECOWAS expressed the commitment of its financial institutions to "… develop policies to facilitate funding for reintegration and reconstruction programmes". Complementarily, Articles 43, 44 and 45 make explicit provisions regarding peace building during and after hostilities and upon the restoration of political authority. Article 44 prescribes activities to be undertaken as part of peace building (recovery from violent conflict), including consolidation of negotiated peace; establishment of conditions for the political, social and economic reconstruction of the society and governmental institutions; implementation of DDR programmes for all categories of combatants; resettlement and assistance to refugees and internally displaced persons; and assistance to vulnerable persons.

Overall, the 1999 protocol encapsulated and documented ECOWAS experiences, lessons, failures and challenges in the formation and deployment of ECOMOG between 1990 and 1998. The provisions of the 1999 protocol were reinforced by the 2001 supplement (Protocol on Democracy and Good Governance) that prescribed the key principles as central elements in conflict prevention, management and peace building. Article 1 of the good governance protocol establishes constitutional convergence principles consistent with the dictates of democratic, liberal precepts, including the constitutional/electoral basis of regime legitimacy and ascension to power, decentralization of power, secularity of the state on matters of religion and fundamental human rights as set out in the relevant UN and OAU charters and rule of law.

The other additions to the peace building architecture in West Africa, especially in the post-1999 period, include close cooperation and partnership between ECOWAS (ECOMOG) and United Nations peace building (peacekeeping) missions in Liberia, Sierra Leone and Côte d'Ivoire. In fact, ECOWAS through ECOMOG spearheaded the increasing involvement of regional organizations in peace building, a practice that has since been replicated and formalized in other parts of the world. Since the 1990s, many sub-regional organizations have exploited Article 52 of the UN Charter that allows states to create regional organizations for dealing with matters of peace and security appropriate for regional action, including enforcement action covered under Chapter VIII of the UN Charter. It was along these lines that the first UN regional office was created in West Africa (UNOWA) to coordinate UN activities and forge a working partnership on peace building with ECOWAS and other stakeholders.[28] UNOWA is also entrusted with promoting a sub-regional approach to peace building through initiatives addressing cross-border insecurity, security sector reform, DDR, youth unemployment and specific intervention in the crises in Côte d'Ivoire and the Bakassi peninsula (between Nigeria and Cameroon).

There have been multiple assistance and training initiatives for the military of ECOWAS member states by major Western countries to enhance their operational capacities and peacekeeping capabilities. The United States initiated the African Crisis Response Initiative (ACRI) (renamed the African Contingency Operations Training and Assistance, ACOTA) to train military trainers and equip African national armies for peace support and humanitarian operations (such as envoy escort, logistics, protection of refugees, command and control and negotiation techniques) thereby increasing their capabilities in human rights, international law and civil-military relations (Howe 2001:19). Klingebiel (2005:38) notes the US's readiness to increase the proportion of its international military assistance budget allocated to Africa, put at over $660 million.

For its part, France has instituted Reinforcing Africa's Capacity to Maintain Peace (RECAMP) and the *Guidimakha* military exercise project to professionalize and build the capacity of African militaries to achieve the similar objective of empowering African states to undertake peacekeeping and peace building operations (Whiteman and Yates 2004). The participation of ECOWAS member states in these military exercises, as well as the institutionalization of ECOMOG, is also being linked organically to the African Union (AU) Peace and Security architecture founded on the creation of an African Standby Force (ASF) composed of five brigades from each of the continent's Regional Economic Communities (RECs) in 2010 (Adebajo 2005:86). ECOWAS is positioning ECOMOG to provide the brigade from West Africa (Sawyer 2005:144).

In spite of West Africa's lead in institutional and legal reforms to reflect the changed security environment and unprecedented challenges of peace building in the post-Cold War era, it is pertinent to highlight four important observations and limitations of contemporary peace building architecture in the sub-region. First is the overt attention and perhaps obsession with the military intervention and peacekeeping component of peace building. This does not preclude the provision of mediation as a conflict resolution strategy. However, ECOWAS's intervention and conflict management roles appear to be built around ECOMOG, not least the elaborate plans for its command structure, composition and deployment under the 1999 protocol. Whilst it is acknowledged that ECOWAS special envoys have been deployed to mediate in crisis situations across the sub-region, including most recently in Guinea[29] (May 2007), the fact remains that ECOWAS's strategy in crisis situations rests on negotiations and the deployment of ECOMOG. Thus,

---

28. For details on the mandate, projects and activities of UNOWA, see http//www.un.org/unowa.

29. For example, see IRIN News (14 May 2007).

ECOWAS's peace building plan is skewed towards military peacekeepers and their role in maintaining physical security (cessation of direct violence).

There is acknowledgement that the expanded role of peacekeepers includes facilitating elections, restoration of political authority, DDR and aspects of post-conflict reconstruction. Yet it appears that the assumption of the ECOWAS strategy hinges on the conflation and confusion of peacekeeping (even with its expanded definition as peace support operations and integrated missions) with the broad spectrum of peace building, and the expectation that military peacekeepers can undertake the totality of peace building or post-peacekeeping peace building activities (reconciliation, social re-engineering and transformation of structures of violence at grassroots level).

However, mainstream peace research literature shows the immense limitations of peacekeepers undertaking lower-end peace building activities. For instance, Hazen (2007:327), in examining the question of whether peacekeepers can be peace builders, argues that "indeed, while peacekeepers are prime actors in post-conflict situations, they are poorly prepared for peace building tasks and have a poor record on this score".

She highlights two key concerns: the first is in terms of approach. It is contended that "peacekeeping missions are based on the premise of assisting war-torn societies to establish, or re-establish, democratic institutions and market economies. To this end, the benchmark for most peacekeeping missions is the holding of elections or democratic elections" (ibid:328). It is argued that, even with the expanded scope of peacekeeping, the mandates and practice of peacekeeping missions continue to be geared towards correcting the short-term, institutional base of conflict, as opposed to the long-term changes in relationships, attitudes and behaviours associated with the incidence of conflict.

Second is the argument that "peacekeeping missions are not designed for peace building" (ibid:329). If anything, peace building has only emerged as a secondary (not primary) priority for peacekeepers. She concludes, "peacekeepers are not trained in peace building, and often lack the necessary skills, local knowledge, and local languages to conduct peace building activities. Peacekeepers often lack an understanding of the situation or the history of the conflict, reducing their effectiveness in peace building efforts" (ibid). It is noted that this reality is compounded by the increasing complexities and complications of peacekeeping operations and poor inter-agency coordination, a situation that often translates into ad hoc and fire brigade approaches to peace building.

A corollary observation and a further limitation in the peace building architecture in West Africa is the strong emphasis on protecting the "stateness" of ECOWAS member states through the implicit attention to protecting regimes (incumbents of power) or facilitating the appearance of normalcy through numerous mechanisms designed to restore political authority. In Guinea-Bissau, the failed 1999 ECOWAS/ECOMOG intervention was principally to protect the *João* Vieira regime. In Liberia, ECOWAS, constituted itself as the source of legitimacy for various regimes through its constitution of interim governments between 1993 and 1997 and in 2003 (Adebajo 2004a and 2004b; Howe 2001:139).

Similarly, the initial intervention in Sierra Leone was to protect the Tejan Kabbah regime. This observation is also underlined by the emphasis in ECOWAS's statutes on zero-tolerance for unconstitutional take-overs of power. In relation to post-conflict situations, this approach is manifest in ECOMOG's primary task of restoring political authority, as noted under Article 45 of the 1999 protocol on conflict management. The strategic objective of protecting, creating or institutionalizing regimes in post-conflict settings is undoubtedly an important goal, but also raises questions about the deepening of peace building. In fact, this approach seems to reaffirm my earlier observation that contemporary peace building is about stability, not change, and security as opposed to peace.

As argued in the previous section, peace building involves, but is not limited to institutional rebuilding or the securing of consensus among power elites or the restoration of political authority. The entire ECOWAS peace building strategy is silent (and the organization lacks any coherent policy or strategy) on civilian peace building and intervention beyond the macro (elite) level. For instance, all the post-accord tasks listed under Article 44(a–e) revolve around activities that fall under the post-conflict reconstruction aspect of peace building. The peace building mechanism is silent on reconciliation at the local communal level, and the process of transforming prewar practices, actors and institutions. Although the decentralization of political authority is emphasized, how this relates to, or affects customary authority and practices at the local level is not addressed. This observation is even more pertinent considering the perversion of democratization processes, manifested in electoral and authoritarian democracies in a majority of countries in West Africa. Thus, the rebuilding of institutions, the restoration of democratic elected regimes, signing and accession to major liberal treaties and principles, and the appearance and observation of other democratic rituals hardly mean the transformation of conflictual relationships and violent structures at sub-national levels. Moreover, democracy and democratization hardly preclude violence.[30] This underlines Mbembe's contention that political transition in a majority of African countries is largely the merely political recomposition of the actors, dynamics and nature of power elites, as opposed to democratic transition and genuine progress along the democratic continuum.[31]

Potentially, some of the normative elements of emergent statutes (on democracy and good governance) do contain important principles. The lack of any institutional mechanisms for monitoring and evaluating these by ECOWAS raises questions about their value beyond official declaration and rhetoric. It is this limitation that underlies the ease with which Liberia relapsed into civil war after the 1996-97 peace process whereby Charles Taylor either retained or remodified post-election institutions, practices and relationships to conform to his wartime preferences. For instance, his dreaded wartime combat groups, including the Small Boys Unit (SBU), were redesignated as official security forces, especially the Anti-Terrorist Unit (ATU), and used to harass and persecute political opponents

---

30. For extensive discourse of violence and democracy, see Keane (2004) and Ross (2004), for example.
31. Mbembe, cited in Joseph (1999:60).

after his election as President. Regrettably, the lesson from Liberia was not reflected in the 1999 protocol.

The third observation about and limitation of peace building in West Africa relates to the ownership, strategic vision and direction of the process. On the one hand, the informalized division of labour, wherein states and organizations (ECOWAS/ECOMOG) in Africa provide the manpower, mainly military peacekeepers, for peace building missions means very little capacity for other peace building activities beyond securing negative peace. This is reinforced by the military training schemes for African countries (including ECOWAS member states) to institutionalize, routinize and restrict their role in peace building to negative peace. As such, ECOWAS has no mechanism, institution or coherent policy to engage with peace building in post-conflict settings after the withdrawal of peacekeeping missions.

On the other hand, the timing, decision on entry and exit strategies, legitimacy, financing and coordination of peace building (including peacekeeping and post-conflict reconstruction) activities are undertaken by extra-African institutions and actors. Beyond the early phase of ECOMOG operations in Liberia (1991–96) and the return to democratic governance in Nigeria in 1999, ECOMOG[32] has not been able to institute any peace building mission independent of UN support. More recent interventions in Sierra Leone, Liberia and Côte d'Ivoire have been spearheaded (including taking strategic decisions) by major Western countries with substantial socioeconomic, cultural, political and historical ties: Britain in Sierra Leone, France in Côte d'Ivoire and the United States in Liberia. In these cases, the lead-Western country largely influenced and assumed important responsibilities for peace building activities, including security sector reform and political and governance reform. In Sierra Leone, Britain assumed responsibilities for security sector reform through the British Military Advisory and Training Teams (BMATT), while the United States did the same in Liberia (this provision was inscribed in the 2003 Comprehensive Peace Agreement).[33]

In certain circumstances, security officials from these Western countries assume direct headship of strategic institutions in economic, security and even judicial areas. For instance, a British police officer headed the Sierra Leonean Police (SLP) as part of the largely British-funded police reform and training programme. To this extent, ECOWAS's presence, role and influence in strategic agenda-setting and implementation in post-conflict settings in the sub-region appears minimal in some regards. It is not unexpected that most peace processes in West Africa appear to conform to a particular (liberal peace) template, marked by power-sharing agreements between fac-

---

32. Olonisakin (2000) notes that military regimes in Nigeria, especially the Babangida and Abacha regimes, hugely facilitated the birth of, and shouldered the massive financial burdens of ECOMOG operations in the early phases for a variety of reasons, including to deflect Western criticism of their domestic authoritarian rule, human rights violations and flawed political transition agenda. Since the return to electoral democracy in 1999, Nigeria has been less willing to shoulder the financial burden of ECOMOG.

33. Part 4 of the 2003 Comprehensive Peace Agreement provides that "the Parties request that ECOWAS, the UN, AU, and the ICG provide advisory staff, equipment, logistics and experienced trainers for the security reform effort. The Parties also request that the United States of America play a lead role in organising this restructuring program".

tions (power elites), elections, security sector reform, the liberalization of economies, truth commissions and criminal courts.[34]

The issue of ownership, control and implementation of peace building (especially components such as reconciliation and social re-engineering) is admittedly contentious. Hazen (2007) argues that non-military peace building is best undertaken by national governments to enhance local ownership, control and direction of the process. It is the contention here, however, that the weakened institutional, financial and political base of most governments in post-conflict settings precludes their exclusive right to undertake peace building. In certain contexts, national regimes could manipulate the process to reward wartime or election allies, or reposition themselves for re-election and thereby cement their sociopolitical power base. This was the case in Liberia under Charles Taylor: the government exploited the process to harass, intimidate and persecute wartime and political opponents. As such, peace building could be enhanced if undertaken by a partnership of national, regional and international actors and institutions.

The foregoing has highlighted some of ECOWAS's limitations as well as its efforts to shore-up its peace building capacity. In June 2007, it kick-started the ECOWAS Conflict Prevention Framework[35] (ECPF) designed to pay more attention to positive peace through a more comprehensive peace building strategy in post-conflict and non-conflict settings. The draft framework called for civilian peacekeeping and emergency response teams and the widening of the role of civil society groups (under the aegis of the West African Civil Society Forum – WACSOF) and the private sector in peace building. It also contained provisions for a sub-regional approach to peace building through attempts to integrate national policies and programmes on youth and gender empowerment. Overall, the ECPF sought to interlock all extant protocols on development and security into a comprehensive peace building strategy.

The draft ECPF is founded more on conflict prevention and less on transformation. This is clear from the declared focus of the ECPF on operational conflict prevention, involving initiatives on early warning, preventive diplomacy, natural resource governance, cross-border insecurity, peace education and tackling youth crises. While most of these initiatives are relevant to sustainable peace across the sub-region, including post-conflict settings, they are, however, still thin on specific strategies and mechanisms for change in post-conflict settings. More importantly, ECOWAS is still beset by massive institutional capacity limitations connected to poor finance, weak internal coordination, piecemeal implementation of programmes, underutilization and misdirection of existing capacity and tensions and weak distribution of roles and responsibilities among ECOWAS, member states, civil society and extra-regional partners.[36] All these factors are likely

---

34. For example, see details of Liberia's post-conflict poverty reduction strategy (postwar socioeconomic and political recovery plan), where these initiatives are clearly stated. See Republic of Liberia (2006).

35. Discussions about the ECPF are from the proceedings of the Workshop "Towards the ECOWAS Strategic Framework for Conflict Prevention", Banjul, The Gambia, 24-28 June 2007. Official restrictions on the circulated draft document prevent any direct citations.

36. Telephone interview with the ECOWAS conflict advisor and coordinator of the ECPF process, 24 September 2007. See also, Jonah (2004).

to increase the tendency towards ad hocism, over-politicization and donor-driven agendas.[37] Moreover, a former Liberian head of state, Amos Sawyer (2005:160), doubts the potential, especially for local populations, of recent and ongoing ECOWAS institutional retooling (including the ECPF) on the basis of its restriction to government-to-government interaction:

> While it is true that these institutions are best provided under the leadership of national governments, a shortcoming is that they are being established largely as undertakings of national governments with little input from the people of West African societies ... Regional systems of justice, security and lawmaking among other systems that affect local populations, need to be considered legitimate by local people if they are to work well.

Back to Praxis: The Un-making of Peace Building in Sierra Leone

In March 1991, a group of fighters loyal to the Charles Taylor-led National Patriotic Front of Liberia (NPFL) crossed into Sierra Leone to effectively kick-start a second war front and bring down what was left of the state of Sierra Leone after years of dysfunctional governance. The group later crystallized into the Revolutionary United Front (RUF) under the political leadership of Corporal Foday Sankoh, a former photographer with the Sierra Leonean army. The RUF rebellion was to destabilize Sierra Leone and the immediate sub-region following many episodes of failed negotiations, agreements, collaboration and interventions. The objective here is not to replicate the discourse about the root causes of the civil war in Sierra Leone,[38] but to examine the extent to which peacekeeping and peace building interventions go beyond the achievement of negative peace to kick-start or transform structural violence inherent in certain social relationships and interactions.

It is worth emphasizing that Sierra Leone was unique in the sense that all through the civil war there was always a regime in power, including the democratically elected Kabbah government. It is important to highlight the causal elements in Sierra Leone's implosion to include systemic (institutional) and structural (relational) factors. These aetiological factors include endemic corruption by government and power elites, bad governance, human rights violations, political oppression and marginalization of opposition and youth, a dysfunctional and over-politicized local governance structure, sub-regional power dynamics and decayed state institutional capacity. The threat and eventual sacking of the Kabbah government in 1997 by a coalition of military officers of the Republic of Sierra Leone Armed Forces (RSLAF) led by Major Paul Koroma and the RUF occasioned the first ECOWAS intervention through a Nigerian-led detachment of ECOMOG soldiers (peacekeepers) in 1997. There followed the restoration of the Kabbah government in 1998 and a re-negotiated peace agreement (Lome Peace Agreement) in 1999. The peace terms, as noted earlier, were effectively a power-

---

37. Ibid.

38. For an extended discussion of the civil war in Sierra Leone, see Richards (1995 and 1996), Richards and Peters (1998), Abdullah (1995 and 2005), Abdullah and Muana (1998), Boas (2007), Keen (2003 and 2007), Reno (1998 and 2003), etc.

sharing agreement between the Kabbah government and the RUF. Under its terms, Kabbah was compelled to cede control of the country's mineral resources (diamonds) to the RUF, as well as grant the RUF rebels total amnesty.

The UN Security Council established the UN Mission in Sierra Leone (UNAMSIL) in October 1999 through Resolution 1270 to facilitate and implement the terms of the Lome Peace Agreement and replace (subsume) ECOMOG operations in Sierra Leone. UNAMSIL stayed in Sierra Leone till December 2005, a five-year period of dithering, inaction, confusion and highs and lows, including the taking hostage of UN peacekeepers, direct unilateral use of force by a separate British military contingent (against the West-Side Boys, a faction of the RUF), and the re-election of Kabbah in May 2002 among others.

At its peak, UNAMSIL had 17,500 peacekeepers, making it one of the largest peace missions in UN history. The "peaceful" (negotiated) end of the conflict and restoration of governmental authority under UNAMSIL, as well as the mission's expanded tasks have often led to its being described as a successful and model mission (Olonisakin 2008:115). Yet the withdrawal of UNAMSIL in 2005 raises a crucial question (already raised in previous sections of this essay): what was achieved in Sierra Leone – negative or positive peace? Underlying this key question are other considerations, including: how appropriate is the five-year window for peace building? What and how was peace building conceived and practised in relation to peacekeeping? Who performed peace building – military or civilian or a combination of both? What informed the exit of UNAMSIL and did it signal the exit of other peace building units, activities and interest?

It is the contention here that only negative peace and regime stability were achieved in Sierra Leone. The exit of UNAMSIL effectively reduced the appropriate level of interest and commitment to peace building. Thus, peace building was largely interpreted in terms of post-conflict reconstruction. While external actors (excluding ECOWAS) ran the show, the national government in Sierra Leone manipulated the process to cement its power base. In this regard, prewar, wartime and postwar relationships remained similarly tense, conflictual and antithetical to peace. It is worth restating that the peace building framework in Sierra Leone revolved around the predetermined logic of "implementing an operational checklist involving fixes to various institutions and processes, without tackling underlying political dynamics" (ICG 2004:1).

The key pillars of these tick-boxes were deployment of peacekeepers (UNAMSIL); undertaking disarmament, demobilization and reintegration of ex-fighters; judicial and security sector reform; economic adjustment and reform conditionalities to facilitate development aid and assistance packages; and elections (ibid). For instance, the judicial reform resulted in the establishment of Truth and Reconciliation Commission (TRC), and an American-sponsored hybrid criminal court. The British administered the Security Sector Reform (SSR) programme as a form of shock therapy to clone a new security apparatus amenable to the democratic ethos and (democratic) civilian oversight. The electoral process in 2002 was heavily encouraged (helping RUF become a registered political party and field a presidential candidate), financed and even conducted by interveners. The economic framework was reoriented even more heavily towards a private sector model, with liberalization of trade, spending caps on various sectors (including key socioeconomic areas of education and health) to achieve macroeconomic stability and the reduced role (reduced to licensing and regulation) of the state in mineral exploitation, especially alluvial diamond mining.

At the onset of UNAMSIL's draw down in December 2004, the key benchmarks for withdrawal were laid down by UNAMSIL's high command and the UN country team. The markers were in five sectors: first was security (cessation and reduced risks of relapse into macro-violence) through appreciable progress in strengthening the office and institutions of national security and rebuilding the armed forces through training and re-equipment. The second was the consolidation of peace and political stability through the promotion of national reconciliation and dialogue, capacity building for parliament and enhanced cooperation for sub-regional initiatives. The third was the consolidation of state authority and governance through support and progress in electoral reform, political devolution and decentralization, enhanced dispensation of justice and government control of areas and operations in diamond mining. The fourth was the successful reintegration of former combatants through community-based (rather than appearing to reward fighters for wartime roles) reintegration, skills development and acquisition programmes for youth, and cross-border initiatives on curbing small arms proliferation, movement of dissidents, and the resettlement of refugees and internally displaced persons.

The last point was the drawing-up and commenced implementation of a national recovery and economic and social development programme aimed at improving economic and financial management, a poverty alleviation strategy, job creation and micro enterprise for youth and support for marginalized groups (women).[39] Although these pillars were originally intended to move from peacekeeping to peace building, the range of non-military issues included and the expanded role and mandate of UNAMSIL (including a fairly big civilian component/staff) appear to suggest it (UNAMSIL) was actually the peace building framework, and that peacekeeping and peace building were conflated and confused. While the UN Peace building Commission succeeded UNAMSIL in January 2006, the initial lack of clarity on its role and mandate, the absence of a coherent and comprehensive framework of engagement and vision of peace building, and its penchant for technical administrative and operational procedures served to indicate at least three things. First is the continued embedding of peace building in peacekeeping as opposed to peacekeeping being seen as a phase along the peace building continuum. This suggests the continued negative impact of the conceptual maze associated with peace building. Second is the relative inexperience and underdevelopment of the global peace building (specifically the non-military components) architecture and the tough challenges that confront it and third is the reality that UNAMSIL's withdrawal

---

39. The five benchmarks are reproduced in Olonisakin (2008:127–8).

was likely to close the peacekeeping (and by extension, peace building) chapter in Sierra Leone.

On benchmarks, Olonisakin's succinct observation in her *Peacekeeping in Sierra Leone: The Story of UNAMSIL* is quite correct – that the benchmark was "an ambitious plan, but it lacked a proper implementation strategy and seemed most concerned with establishing benchmarks and ticking them off before December 2005 in order to demonstrate UNAMSIL's success. The time period was of course hopelessly unrealistic" (2008:126). She concludes that, "in the end, security was the only withdrawal benchmark achieved with a high degree of satisfaction by the time UNAMSIL's mandate formally ended in December 2005" (ibid). Similarly, Hazen, (2007:330) in interrogating peace building in Sierra Leone, raised crucial questions on whether UNAMSIL, whose role, mandate and institutional design suggested it was meant to be a peacekeeping-peace building mission, was able to address the underlying causes of the conflict, institute non-violent ways of managing social conflicts and transform attitudes that favour violent action for social change. She concludes that:

> ... evidence suggests that the peacekeeping mission was able to greatly reduce violence in order to provide an enabling environment for national actors to begin a peace building process, but that UNAMSIL did not achieve significant progress on other fronts. Upon its departure in late December 2005, peace building remained in its early stages, institutions remained weak, attitudes remained unchanged and the underlying causes of the conflict remained largely unaddressed.

The reviews of the benchmarks either as a withdrawal plan or peace building framework do not confirm their utility in achieving sustainable, positive peace (Forman 2002): rather the reviews underline confusion, ad hocism and a lack of clarity of roles and responsibilities for different actors and stakeholders, all alluded to by Olonisakin (2008). The failure in non-hardware security tasks of peace building appears to be highlighted in the National Recovery Strategy (NRS) for Sierra Leone (2002–03). The NRS was "designed to form a bridge between emergency intervention and long term development and aims to engage Sierra Leonean society in the reconciliation and democratization process" (NRS 2002:9). The strategy also declared that "it is also aimed at promoting a people-centred approach seeking community empowerment and participation. Indeed, although much infrastructure has to be reconstructed or rehabilitated, the focus and priorities of the strategy are as much about human resources and capacity building as they are about physical infrastructure" (ibid). The NRS listed four priority areas of intervention: restoration of state authority to provide security, law and order, policy, coordination and control of economic resources; rebuilding communities through resettlement of displaced people and refugees and reintegration of ex-fighters; peace building and human rights by building capacity for peaceful conflict resolution and reconciliation in society; and the restoration of the economy through enhanced economic growth and revenue for facilitate service delivery (ibid:17).

In spite of the obvious importance of the NRS goals to sustainable peace, virtually all its programme areas were either not funded or received little funding, with initiatives relating to deepening peace building (achieving positive peace) as the greatest casualty. Of course, much of the funding and financing of peace building activities are usually expected to come from external sources, principally richer Western countries. The "beggarly" situation of governments in most post-conflict settings, including Western Europe after World War II under the Marshall Plan, renders them vulnerable to the dictates of third party actors with the financial resources to influence or even determine the substantive elements and direction of postwar reconstruction efforts.[40] Hence, the non-funding of certain activities raises questions about the overall aim of intervention and the type of peace desired, thus buttressing the argument on stability versus change, and security versus peace.

In Sierra Leone, the programme for the consolidation of state authority attracted only about 30% ($3.12 million) of the needed $12.3 million, leaving a shortfall of over $9 million (NRS 2002:18). Of this, the funding for the deployment of district officials to enhance the governmental presence in the provinces received less than $1 million of the needed $5.6 million (ibid: 19). Strengthening the police force (outside the SSR programme of the British) had a funding commitment of over $1.1 million of the total $1.9 million (nearly 60% of funding secured), while that for judicial reform only had $50,000 of the required $761,500 (a shortfall of over 90%) (ibid:19). The prison reform programme also had a shortfall of nearly 70%.

---

40. For extended discussion on the Marshall Plan and the history of postwar reconstruction, see Williams (2005), Ugo (1947) and Henry (1942).

On the reintegration of ex-combatants, UNAMSIL DDR statistics showed that over 42,000 weapons were collected and nearly 75,000 fighters were demobilized. However, the NRS noted the huge challenge of moving from demobilization to reintegration, with over 23,000 caseloads (ex-combatants needing reintegration assistance), a majority of whom were concentrated in the highly volatile and precarious Kailahun district. The reintegration programme was and continues to be beset by problems of limited in-country implementation capacity, slow deployment of implementing partners to locations, increased cost of engaging capable agencies, slow expansion of the economy to generate private sector employment, and a massive funding shortfall of over $11 million for reintegration services (NRS 2002:30). Thus, while the disarmament and demobilization programmes undertaken by UNAMSIL were heavily financed, the reintegration phase faced a funding shortfall of over 70% (ibid).

Even the critical peace building and human rights component of the national recovery strategy attracted minimal funding – of the almost $2 million needed, only $704,000 (representing about 35%) was committed (NRS 2002:47). However, on the economic front, of the needed $139 million for economic restoration at the macro-level, an impressive $82.3 million (representing 60%) was committed, in addition to another $72.3 million for transport infrastructure development. But the micro-level programmes, such as a micro-finance programme, had no funding commitments for the needed $1.2 million (NRS 2002: 48–58). Similarly, of the $30 million plus needed for jump-starting agricultural production of food crops, cash crop plantations, livestock and fisheries, only $10 million (representing 33%) was committed.[41] The rebuilding of educational infrastructure and training of teachers, a key service for youth (including former combatants), attracted $6.9 million (representing about 40%) of the needed $15.5 million (ibid).

Overall, the NRS budgeted $212.5 million but only attracted funding commitments for $115.8 million, leaving a shortfall of over $102 million (representing a shortfall of nearly 50%) (ibid). One noticeable pattern in the funding for the NRS was the tendency for macro-level and more security hardware-related issues (connected to regime stability)[42] to be better funded than micro-level initiatives (with minimal tendency to upset regime security). That the NRS received minimal funding in 2003 when Sierra Leone was highly coveted and enjoyed considerable international goodwill as a "success story" was already bad enough. To further worsen the problem, UNAMSIL left the country. The limited funding for lower-end (non-military) aspects, as well as overall under-funding of peace building in Africa by Western countries underscores the reality that geopolitical considerations, as opposed to humanitarian ones are writ large in such interventions. For instance, American Congresswoman Cynthia McKinney in 2000 noted that the pressure on the Kabbah government and ECOWAS to negotiate and conclude a power-sharing agreement with the RUF was an indication that the US was unwilling to, and never provided meaningful assistance to ECOMOG. It can also be noted that while the US provided an average of $4 million to ECOMOG in 1999, it spent over $60 million per day in peace operations (bombing) in Serbia, and made only a $15 million long term funding commitment to ECOMOG/UN operations in Sierra Leone, while a downpayment of $13 billion was committed for NATO/EU/UN peace operations in Kosovo (cited in Abraham 2000:23).

To further underscore the point about the primacy of geopolitical interests, it is worth acknowledging that, over the three years since the withdrawal of UNAMSIL and the down-scaling of the repertoire of other elements of the peace building complex (aid and development agencies, etc) in Sierra Leone, the EU/UN range of peace builders (military and civilian) are still deployed in Kosovo and there is as yet no serious discussion of their withdrawal and exit strategy.[43] The tailoring of peace building agendas to the priorities (including catchy and headline-grabbing issues) of external actors is also reflected in the favourable funding of the International Criminal Court in Freetown

---

41. See appendix to the NRS (2002).
42. My claim here does not preclude teething problems in the macro-level initiatives, such as the security sector reform programme that suffered from inefficient training, little attention to capacity in other government agencies in respect of oversight of the security forces, little public confidence in the security forces, and the predominance of external actors in planning and the implications thereof, including appointments into commanding positions. For details of SSR in post-conflict peace building, see Gbla (2006) and Brzoka (2006).

43. The five-year deployment of UNAMSIL and withdrawal in 2005 does not include Britain's 10-year commitment to provide development assistance to Sierra Leone. However, this still falls short of the 25-year peace building window advocated, for example, by the International Crisis Group. See ICG (2004).

largely by Washington, while national judicial reform was stalled and underfunded. Hazen (2007:332), for instance, notes that "the judicial system in Sierra Leone offered little in the way of efficient, equitable, or timely conflict resolution. There was no comprehensive reform programme in place to address the lack of capacity, independence, impartiality and access. The judicial system remained extremely weak".

The foregoing shortfalls, as well as the failure to deepen peace building, appear not to engender regime stability and security, at least in the short term. However, they have substantial implications for regime sustainability in the long term, as well as huge implications already for human security, socioeconomic development and good governance. In previous research on the reintegration of young combatants in Sierra Leone, I noted similar systematic failures in the disarmament, demobilization and socioeconomic reintegration of former youth fighters and its manifest effects (Ismail 2003). For instance, the child combatant component of the DDR was flawed in several respects, including the use of certain criteria (such as the presentation of, and the demonstration of the ability to assemble and dismantle) weapons, and excluded a considerable number of child soldiers. Some child fighters who had been indirectly involved in the war as spies, camp followers and load carriers, for instance, were incapable of presenting or operating any weapon. This criterion also excluded many girls who were cooks, domestic servants, wives and sexual toys for commandos. Also, the use of group disarmament in phases II and III of the DDR process worked to exclude child fighters by placing commandos at the heart of the DDR (whereby they negotiated the number of fighters under their command with DDR officials), with the result that only those declared or presented by commandos were registered as combatants. But with DDR benefits (especially an initial package of *Le*300, 000) awaiting adult fighters, commandos resorted to presenting (hiring) non-combatant adults, rather than turning in actual child fighters. As such, the 6,845 child fighters disarmed and demobilized did not reflect the reality of over 10,000 former child fighters.

The study also noted that the reintegration of young combatants was stalled as a result of funding and other problems. In the first instance, the mainly community based reintegration model employed meant that only former young combatants within families and communities benefited. Second, the Community Education Investment Program (CEIP) and the Complimentary Rapid Education Primary School (CREPS) launched to cater for the educational needs of different classes of demobilized young people was undercut by funding. Dilapidated classrooms and acute shortages of teaching materials and personnel, for example, largely paralyzed the CEIP.

The vocational skills-training programme suffered from practical (implementation) problems ranging from inadequate finance and training materials to the provision of skills whose economic viability in the local economy is limited. Not unexpectedly, a high percentage of graduates from the skills training programmes were prone to selling off the start-up kits given to them or completely abandoned practising the trades they had learned.

The study also related these failures to the quadrupled number of street *Pikin*[44] in urban centres, especially Freetown (in places such as *Sawpit, Big Wharf, Salad Ground, PZ, Kola Store, Aberdeen, Lumley Podapoda Parks,* and *Victoria Park*), in the postwar period. This has resulted in a corresponding increase in crime, including rape, burglaries, prostitution, theft and armed robberies.

Similarly, Fanthorpe (2005) in his review of governance reform, especially political decentralization, noted the competing interests between external (Western, liberal peace) and national elites (government) over the chieftaincy system. The former, on account of their view of the chieftaincy system as "backward" (hence the need for "modernization") and the assumed complicity of local chiefs and culture in the atrocities committed during the civil war, pushed for a completely new system in which all local administrators were to be elected (truly representative). In contrast, the latter remained supportive of the chieftaincy system, not least to cement their political power base. The reform programme for decentralization undertaken under the Paramount Chiefs Restoration Programme (PCRP) was funded by the British Department for International Development (DfID).

Fanthorpe notes that a combination of manipulation and resistance by national elites (government) has led to a complicated two-tier system that signposts political accommodation rather than efficiency. Thus, donors continue to deal with the new district councils that have been designated as the implementation institutions for post-conflict reconstruction at the grassroots level. The government, on the other hand, deals with chieftaincies to administer customary law and maintain general order in the provinces. Fanthorpe also noted that contrary to the outsiders' general impression, the chieftaincy system was still popular among local inhabitants in the interpretation of customary property rights and citizenship. He states that the prewar complicity of chieftaincies needed to be understood in the context of over-politicization of the chieftaincy system by the power elite (nothing was wrong with it as a system of local administration), and inadequate financing by central authorities. He concludes that the prioritization of the interest of macro actors (donors and national power elites) has created a tense and complicated system of local administration in postwar Sierra Leone. Of relevance is his observation that prewar and wartime patterns of over-politicizing the chieftaincy system were returning – for instance, he cites cases of duplication of duties and multiple taxation involving the district councils and chiefdom administrations, thereby impoverishing local inhabitants (Fanthorpe 2005:46). He also notes that, reminiscent of prewar practices under the All People's Congress (APC) regime:

> ... several paramount chiefs campaigned actively in the run up to the May 2004 elections, most on behalf of the SLPP. An allegation circulating widely during this period was that the government would depose chiefs who failed to support the ruling party and/or its official candidates and that paramount chiefs would do the same to section chiefs who failed to support their party of choice ... elsewhere, there have been reports of

---

44. This is a generic term for the urban marginals and street children/youth that roam the major business centres and markets in Freetown.

newly elected district councillors allying with chiefdom political factions in attempts to create spheres of authority that specifically exclud

The evidence and information suggest the failure to transform the oppressive and violent structures that permeated government and society in the prewar years. The ICG in 2002 noted that issues critical to sustainable peace building (and needing to be addressed) include a fair electoral system devoid of force, fraud and violence; geo-ethnic divides and tensions between the Temne (North) and Mende (South); the "winner-takes-all" approach to political and electoral competition; and endemic corruption at all levels of government (ICG 2002). In 2003, the think tank in its evaluation of governance and security noted the stagnation of reform programmes, the government's lack of a coherent policy direction and agenda, poor reintegration of ex-combatants, continued illegal alluvial diamond mining (albeit less than in the prewar and wartime period); the stalled anti-corruption campaign (with the Anti-Corruption Commission hamstrung by political interference); and a flawed political decentralization programme. It concluded by noting the gradual reversal of short-term gains occasioned by miniature reform programmes and the alarming drift back to the pre-conflict ways of doing things (ICG 2003).

In the build-up to the 2007 elections, the ICG noted the full-scale return to the pre-conflict practice of violent political and electioneering processes (with the burning of houses in Punjehun district in January 2007, for example); how the reversion to constituency-based voting system for parliament reinforces the leverage and politicization of traditional chiefs in national politics; and the continued marginalization of and attempts to manipulate youth (ICG 2007). Also, in December 2007 the new Ernest Bai Koroma regime, on account of a preliminary audit of government departments, discovered fraud and embezzlement and mismanagement of post-conflict finance and assistance packages in the areas of health, security and tax, and ordered a full-scale probe of officials who had served under the Kabbah regime (BBC, 13 Dec 2007).

Conclusion

This essay has traced the genealogy of contemporary peace building architecture at the global and sub-regional (West African) levels. It argues that contemporary peace building is often confused, conflated with and embedded in peacekeeping. Moreover, global geopolitical dynamics (the end of the Cold War and the onset of the War on Terror for example) and changes in the forms of warfare (new wars) have altered and continue to influence the form, challenges, scope and objectives of peace interventions by Western countries, especially in Africa. A crucial point is that peace building remains largely externally driven, with minimal local participation in the design or ownership of the process.

The paper contends that the conception and practice of contemporary peace building in West Africa is largely skewed towards the domestic and international priorities of interveners, mostly extra-African actors. Therefore, the impact of such interventions includes the alienation of the interests of the masses in post-conflict societies and, worse still, the superficial treatment of the roots of conflict that does not go beyond the stabilization and security of the postwar government. What this does is to increase the risk of the re-integration of post-conflict societies into the vicious cycle of the prewar situation, and the putting at grave risk of an already fragile post-conflict "peace".

It is important to note that the foregoing analysis underscores the organic connections between the meaning, tools and practice of peace building in West Africa (through ECOWAS and its peace building architecture) and global patterns, especially the liberal peace paradigm orthodoxy. Therefore, the extant forms and practices of peace building is the sub-region are more likely to achieve negative peace (cessation of physical violence) because of international humanitarianism, as well as to ensure regime stability that reduces the risk of international terrorism. However, they are unlikely to achieve sustainable peace and transform the structures of violence inherent in certain interactions, sociopolitical relations and practices in the West African sub-region. More studies are needed to explore the potential benefits of indigenous forms of participatory peacemaking and peace building that should emphasize post-conflict transformation based on a genuine democratically rooted praxis and practice that is equally sensitive to issues of civic empowerment, national ownership, capacity-building at all levels and an equitable and sustainable peace.

Bibliography

Abdullah, I. (2005) "'I am a Rebel". Youth Culture and Violence in Sierra Leone'. In A. Honwana and F. De Boeck (eds), *Makers and Breakers: Children and Youth in Postcolonial Africa*. Oxford/Trenton/Dakar: James Currey/Africa World Press/Codesria, pp. 172–87.

Abdullah, I. (1998) 'Bush Path to Destruction: The Origin and Character of the Revolutionary United Front/Sierra Leone', *Journal of Modern African Studies*, 36, 2(1998), pp. 203–35.

Abdullah, I. and P. Muana (1998) 'The Revolutionary United Front of Sierra Leone. A Revolt of the Lumpenproletariat'. In Clapham, C. (ed.), *African Guerillas*. Oxford/Kampala/Bloomington and Indianapolis: James Currey/Fountain Publishers/Indiana University Press, pp. 172–94.

Aboagye, F. (1999) *ECOMOG: A Sub-regional Experience in Conflict Resolution, Management and Peacekeeping in Liberia*, Accra.

Abraham, A. (2000) "The Quest for Peace in Sierra Leone." In *Engaging Sierra Leone, A Report by the Centre for Democracy and Development, London, CDD Strategy Planning Series 4*. London: CDD, pp. 12–36.

Addison, T. (2003) *Africa's Recovery from Conflict: Making Peace Work for the Poor*. Helsinki: UNU-WIDER.

Addison, T. (1998) 'Underdevelopment, Transition and Reconstruction in SSA', *UNU-WIDER Research for Action*, No. 45. Helsinki: UNU-WIDER.

Addison, T. and S.M. Murshed (t2001) 'From Conflict to Reconstruction: Reviving the Social Contract', *UNU-WIDER, Discussion Paper*, No. 2001/48. Helsinki: UNU-WIDER.

Adebajo, A. (2005) 'The Curse of Berlin: Africa's Security Dilemmas', *IPG* 4/2005.

Adebajo, A. (2004) 'Pax West Africana? Regional Security Mechanisms'. In Adebajo, A. And R. Ismail (eds), *West Africa's Security Challenges: Building Peace in A Troubled Region*. Boulder/London: Lynne Rienner for International Peace Academy, pp. 291–318.

Adebajo, A. (2002) 'Liberia: A Warlord's Peace'. In Stedman, J., D. Rothchild and E. Cousens (eds), *Ending Civil Wars: The Implementation of Peace Agreements*. Boulder/London: International Peace Academy and the Centre for International Security and Cooperation: Lynne Rienner, pp. 599–631.

Barnett, M. (2006) 'Building a Republican Peace: Stabilizing States after War', *International Security*, Vol. 30, No. 4, pp. 87–112.

BBC News/Africa, (13 December 2007), "Sierra Leone Orders Corruption Probe", available at http://news.bbc.co.uk/1/hi/world/africa/7141891.stm.

Bellamy, A. (2004) 'The Next Stage in Peace Operations Theory?' *International Peacekeeping*, Vol. 11, No. 1, pp. 17–38.

Bello, W. (2006) 'The Rise of the Relief-and-Reconstruction Complex', Columbia *Journal of International Affairs*, Vol. 59, No. 2, pp. 281–96.

Berdal, M. (1996) 'Disarmament and Demobilisation after Civil Wars', *Adelphi Paper* 303.

Berger, M. (2006) 'From Nation-Building to State-Building: The Geopolitics of Development, the Nation-state System and the Changing Global Order', *Third World Quarterly*, 27(1), pp. 5–25.

Berger, M. and H. Weber (2006) 'Beyond State-Building: Global Governance and the Crisis of the Nation-state System in the 21st Century', *Third World Quarterly*, 27(1), pp. 201–8.

Blagojevic, B. (2007) 'Peacebuilding in Ethnically Divided Societies', *Peace Review*, 19(4), pp. 555–62.

Boas, M. (2007) 'Marginalized Youth'. In Boas, M. and K. Dunn (eds), *African Guerrillas, Raging Against the Machine*. Boulder: Lynne Rienner, pp. 39–54.

Borer, T. (2006) 'Truth Telling as a Peacebuilding Activity: A Theoretical Overview'. In Borer (ed.), *Telling the Truths. Truth Telling and Peace Building in Post-Conflict Societies*. Notre Dame: University of Notre Dame, pp. 1–58.

Borer, T. et al. (2006) *Peacebuilding after Peace Accords: The Challenges of Violence, Truth, and Youth*. Notre Dame:University of Notre Dame Press.

Brzoska, M. (2006) 'Introduction: Criteria for Evaluating Post-Conflict Reconstruction and Security Sector Reform in Peace Support Operations', *International Peacekeeping*, 13(1), pp. 1–13.

Carbonnier, G. (1998) 'Conflict, Post-war Rebuilding and the Economy', *WIDER Occasional Paper* No. 2. Helsinki: WIDER.

Chandler, D. (2004) 'The Responsibility to Protect? Imposing the Liberal Peace', *International Peacekeeping*, Vol. 11, No. 1, pp. 59–81.

Chomsky, N. (2006) *Failed States: The Abuse of Power and Assault on Democracy*. London: Penguin.

Collier, P. (2004) 'Development and Security', Text of Public Lecture Delivered at 12th Bradford Development Lecture, Bradford Centre for International Development, Bradford University, UK, 11 November 2004.

Collier, P. and A. Hoeffler (2002) 'Aid, Policy and Peace: Reducing the Risks of Civil Conflict', *Defence and Peace Economics*, Vol. 13(6), pp. 435–50.

Collier, P. and A. Hoeffler (2001) *Greed and Grievance in Civil Wars*. US/UK: World Bank/CEPHR/CSAE. Available online at www.worldbank.org (search for author-s and title). Accessed 2 December 2003.

Cooper, N. (2005) 'Picking out the Pieces of the Liberal Peaces: Representations of Conflict Economies and the Implications for Policy', *Security Dialogue*, Vol. 36(4), pp. 463–78.

Coyne, C. (2006) 'Reconstructing Weak and Failed States', *The Journal of Social, Political and Economic Studies*, Vol. 31, No. 2 Summer 2006, pp. 143–62.

Curran, D. and T. Woodhouse (2007) 'Cosmopolitan Peacekeeping Peace building in Sierra Leone: What can Africa Contribute?' *International Affairs*, 83(6), pp. 1055–70.

Darby, J. (2006) 'The Post-Accord Context'. In Darby, J. (ed.), *Violence and Reconstruction*. Notre Dame: University of Notre Dame Press, pp. 1–10.

Dobbins, J. et al. (2007) *The Beginner's Guide to Nation-Building*. Santa Monica: RAND.

Dobbins, J. (2004) 'The UN's Role in Nation-building: From the Belgian Congo to Iraq', *Survival* Vol. 46, No. 4, Winter 2004–05, pp. 81–102.

Dobbins, J. (2003) 'America's Role in Nation-building: From Germany to Iraq', *Survival*, Vol. 45, No. 4, Winter 2003–04, pp. 87–110.

Dobbins, J. et al. (2003) *America's Role in Nation-building: From Germany to Iraq*. Santa Monica: RAND.

Dodge, T. (2006) 'Iraq: The Contradictions of Exogenous State-building in Historical Perspective', *Third World Quarterly*, 27(1), pp. 187–200.

Duffield, M. (2007) *Development, Security and Unending War: Governing the World of Peoples*. Cambridge: Polity Press.

Duffield, M. (2005) 'Social Reconstruction: The Reuniting of Aid and Politics', *Development*, 48(3), pp. 16–24.

Duffield, M. (2001) *Global Governance and the New Wars*. London/New York: Zed Books.

Dzelilovic, V. (2002) 'World Bank, NGOs and the Private Sector in Post-war Reconstruction', *International Peacekeeping*, 9(2), pp. 81–98.

ECOWAS (2001) *Protocol A/SP1/12/01 On Democracy and Good Governance*. Abuja: ECOWAS.

ECOWAS (1999) *Protocol Relating to the Mechanism for Conflict Prevention, Management, Resolution, Peacekeeping and Security*. Abuja: ECOWAS.

Edelstein, D. (2004) 'Occupational Hazards: Why Military Occupations Succeed or Fail', *International Security*, 29(1), pp. 49–91.

Etzioni, A. (2004) 'A Self-restrained Approach to Nation-building by Foreign Powers', *International Affairs*, 80(1), pp. 1–17.

Fanthorpe, R. (2005) 'On the Limits of Liberal Peace: Chiefs and Democratic Decentralization in Post-war Sierra Leone', *African Affairs*, 105/148, pp. 27–49.

Fetherston, A.B. (2000) 'Peacekeeping, Conflict Resolution and Peacebuilding: A Reconsideration of Theoretical Frameworks', *International Peacekeeping*, 7(1), pp. 190–218.

Forman, J. (2002) 'Achieving Socio-Economic Well-Being in Post-Conflict Settings', *Washington Quarterly*, 25, Autumn 2002, pp. 125–38.

The Foucault Effect. Hemel Hempstead: Harvester Wheatsheaf, pp. 87–104.

Foucault, M. (1991) 'Questions of Methods'. In Burchill, C., C. Gordon, P. Millar (eds), *The Foucault Effect*. Hemel Hempstead: Harvester Wheatsheaf, pp. 74–86.

Freeman, C. (2007) 'Introduction: Security, Governance and Statebuilding in Afghanistan', *International Peacekeeping*, 14(1), pp. 1–7.

Fukuyama, F. (2006) 'Nation-Building and the Failure of Institutional Memory'. In Fukuyama, F. (ed.), *Nation Building Beyond Afghanistan and Iraq*. Baltimore: Johns Hopkins University Press, pp. 1–18.

Fukuyama, F. (2005) *State-Building: Governance and World Order in the 21ˢᵗ Century*. London: Profile Books.

Galtung, J. (1964) 'A Structural Theory of Aggression', *Journal of Peace Research*, No. 2, pp. 95–119.

Gbla, O. (2006) 'Security Sector Reform under International Tutelage in Sierra Leone', *International Peacekeeping* 13(1), pp. 78–93.

Gennip, J. (2005) 'Post-conflict Reconstruction and Development', *Development* 48(3), pp. 57–62.

Goodhand, J. and M. Sedra (2007) 'Bribes or Bargains? Peace Conditionalities and "Post-Conflict" Reconstruction in Afghanistan', *International Peacekeeping*, Vol. 14, No. 1, pp. 41–61.

Gurr, T. (1970) *Why Men Rebel*. Princeton: Princeton University Press.

Guttal, S. (2005) 'The Politics of Post-war/Post-Conflict Reconstruction', *Development*, 48(3), pp. 73–81.

Hamre, J. and G. Sullivan (2002) 'Towards Post-Conflict Reconstruction', *Washington Quarterly*, 25(2002), pp. 85–96.

Hazen, J. (2007) 'Can Peacekeepers be Peacebuilders?' *International Peacekeeping* Vol. 14, No. 3, pp. 323–38.

Heathershaw, J. (2007) 'Peace building as Practice: Discourses from Post-conflict Tajikistan', *International Peacekeeping*, Vol. 14, No. 2, pp. 219–36.

Henry, P. (ed.), (1942) *Problems of Post War Reconstructio*. Washington: American Council on Public Affairs.

Howe, H. (2001) *Ambiguous Order. Military Forces in African States*. Boulder and London: Lynne Rienner.

ICG (2007) 'Sierra Leone: The Election Opportunity', *Africa Report*, No. 129, 12 July 2007.

ICG (2004) 'Liberia and Sierra Leone: Rebuilding Failed States', *Africa Report*, No. 87, 08 December 2004.

ICG (2003) 'Sierra Leone: The State of Security and Governance', *Africa Report*, No. 67, 02 September 2003.

ICG (2002) 'Sierra Leone after Elections: Politics as Usual?' *Africa Report*, No. 49, 15 July 2002.

IRIN News (14 May 2007) "GUINEA: Soldiers Continue Looting after President Concedes to Demands", http://www.irinnews.org/Report.aspx?ReportId=72138.

Ismail, O. (2003) *The Day After: Child Soldiers in Post-war Sierra Leone*. Report submitted to the SSRC, New York, African Youth in the Era of Globalization Fellowship Programme.

Jonah, J. (2004) The United Nations. in Adebajo, A. and R. Ismail (eds), *West Africa's Security Challenges. Building Peace in a Troubled Region*. Boulder and London: Lynne Rienner, pp. 319–348.

Jones, S. et al. (2005) *Establishing Law and Order after Conflict*. Santa Monica: RAND.

Joseph, R. (1999) 'The Reconfiguration of Power in Late Twentieth-Century Africa'. In Joseph, R. (ed.), *State, Conflict and Democracy in Africa*. Boulder/London: Lynne Rienner, pp. 57–82.

Kaldor, M. (2001) *New and Old Wars: Organized Violence in a Global Era*. Stanford: Stanford University Press.

Kang, S. and J. Meernik (2004) 'Determinants of Post-Conflict Economic Assistance', *Journal of Peace Research*, Vol. 41, No. 2, pp. 149–66.

Keane, J. (2004) *Violence and Democracy*. Cambridge: Cambridge University Press.

Keen, D. (2008) *Complex Emergencies*. London: Polity Press.

Keen, D. (2003) 'Greedy Elites, Dwindling Resources, Alienated Youths: The Anatomy of Protracted Violence in Sierra Leone', *International Politics and Society (IPG)*, 2/2003.

Keen, D. (2000) 'War and Peace: What's the Difference?' *International Peacekeeping*, 7(4), pp. 1–22.

Klingebiel, S. (2005) 'Africa's New Peace and Security Architecture', *African Security Review*, 14(2), pp. 35–44.

Krause, K. and O. Jutersonke (2005) 'Peace, Security and Development in Post-Conflict Environments', *Security Dialogue*, Vol. 36, No.4, pp. 447–62.

Last, D. (2000) in Ramsbotham, O. et al., *The Bergerhof Handbook for Conflict Transformation*. Germany: Bergerhof Research Centre for Constructive Conflict Management.

Lederach, J.P. (2003) *The Little Book of Conflict Transformation*. Intercourse: Good Books.

Malone, D. and K. Wermester (2000) 'Boom and Bust? The Changing Nature of UN Peacekeeping', *International Peacekeeping*, 7(4), pp. 37–54.

Mani, R. (2005) 'Balancing Peace with Justice in the Aftermath of Violent Conflict', *Development* 48(3), pp. 25–34.

Mani, R. (2005) 'Rebuilding an Inclusive Political Community after War', *Security Dialogue*, Vol. 36(4), pp. 511–26.

McEvoy-Levy, S. (2006) 'Introduction: Youth and the Post-Accord Environment'. In McEvoy-Levy, S. (ed.), *Troublemakers or Peacemakers? Youth and Post-Accord Peace Building*. Notre Dame: University of Notre Dame, pp. 1–26.

McMullin, J. (2004) 'Reintegration of Combatants: Were the Right Lessons Learned in Mozambique?' *International Peacekeeping*, Vol. 11, No. 4, pp. 625–43.

Miall, H. et al. (1999) *Contemporary Conflict Resolution*. London: Polity Press.

Montgomery, J. and D. Rondinelli (2004) 'A Path to Reconstruction: Proverbs of Nation-building', *Harvard International Review*, Summer 2004, pp. 26–9.

Moran, M. (2006) *Liberia: The Violence of Democracy*. Philadelphia: University of Pennsylvania Press.

National Recovery Strategy (NRS) Sierra Leone 2002–2003 (n.d).

Natsios, A. (2005) 'The Nine Principles of Reconstruction and Development', *Parameters*, Autumn 2005, pp. 4–20.

Nitzschke, H. and K. Studdard (2005) 'The Legacies of War Economies: Challenges and Options for Peacemaking and Peace building', *International Peacekeeping*, Vol. 12, No. 2, pp. 222–39.

Olonisakin, F. (2008) *Peacekeeping in Sierra Leone: The Story of UNAMSIL*. Boulder/London: Lynne Rienner for International Peace Academy.

Olonisakin, F. (2000) 'Reinventing Peacekeeping in Africa. Conceptual and Legal Issues in ECOMOG Operations'. Hague/London/Boston: Kluwer Law International.

Paris, R. (2004) *At War's End: Building Peace after Civil Conflict*. New York: Cambridge University Press.

Pearce, J. (2005) 'The International Community and Peacebuilding', *Development* 48(3), pp. 41–9.

Peters, K. and P. Richards (1998) 'Why We Fight: Voices of Youth Combatants in Sierra Leone', *Africa*, Vol. 68, No. 2, pp. 183–210.

Plattner, M. (2005) 'Building Democracy after Conflict: Introduction', *Journal of Democracy*, Vol. 16, No. 1, pp. 5–8.

Poku, N. et al. (2007) 'Human Security and Development in Africa', *International Affairs* 83(6), pp. 1155–70.

Pouligny, B. (2005) 'Civil Society and Post-Conflict Peacebuilding: Ambiguities of International Programmes Aimed at Building "New" Societies', *Security Dialogue* Vol. 36(4), pp. 495–510.

Pugh, M. (2004) 'Peacekeeping and Critical Theory', *International Peacekeeping*, Vol. 11, No. 1, pp. 39–58.

Ramsbotham, O. (2000) 'Reflections on UN Post-Settlement Peacebuilding', *International Peacekeeping*, 7(1), pp. 169–89.

Reilly, B. (2002) 'Post-Conflict Elections: Constraints and Dangers', *International Peacekeeping*, 9(2), pp. 118–39.

Reno, W. (2003) 'Political Networks in a Failing State: The Roots and Future of Violent Conflict in Sierra Leone', *International Politics and Society (IPG)*, 2/2003.

Reno, W. (1998) *Warlord Politics and African States*. Boulder: Lynne Rienner.

Republic of Liberia (n.d.) *Interim Poverty Reduction Strategy. Breaking with the Past: From Conflict to Development*. Liberia.

Richards, P. (1995) 'Rebellion in Liberia and Sierra Leone: A Crisis of Youth?' In Furley, O. (ed.), *Conflict in Africa*. London/New York: Tauris, pp. 134–70.

Richards, P. (1996) *Fighting for the Rain Forest: War Youth and Resources in Sierra Leone*. London: International African Institute and James Currey.

Richmond, O. (2004) 'UN Peace Operations and the Dilemmas of the Peacebuilding Consensus', *International Peacekeeping* 11(1), pp. 83–101.

Ross, D. (2004) *Violent Democracy*, Cambridge: Cambridge University Press.

Rubinstein, R. (2005) 'Intervention and Culture: An Anthropological Approach to Peace Operations', *Security Dialogue*, Vol. 36, No. 4, pp. 527–44.

Runciman, W. (1966) *Relative Deprivation and Social Justice*. London: Routledge and Kegan Paul.

Ryan, S. (2000) 'United Nations Peacekeeping: A Matter of Principles?' *International Peacekeeping*, 7(1), pp. 27–47.

Sawyer, A. (2005) *Beyond Plunder: Towards Democratic Governance in Liberia*. Boulder/London: Lynne Rienner.

Schnabel, A. (2002) 'Post-Conflict Peacebuilding and Second-Generation Preventive Action', *International Peacekeeping*, 9(2), pp. 7–30.

Schwarz, R. (2005) 'Post-Conflict Peacebuilding: The Challenges of Security, Welfare and Representation', *Security Dialogue*, Vol. 36, No. 4, pp. 429–46.

Simonsen, S. (2004) 'Nation-building as Peacebuilding: Racing to Define the Kosovar', *International Peacekeeping*, 11(2), pp. 289–311.

SIPRI (2002) *SIPRI Year Book 2002: Armaments, Disarmament and International Security*. Oxford: Oxford University Press.

Sorensen, B. (1998) Women and Post-Conflict Reconstruction, *WIDER Occasional Paper No. 3*. Geneva: WIDER.

Sriram, C. (2000) 'Truth Commissions and the Quest for Justice: Stability and Accountability after Internal Strife', *International Peacekeeping*, 7(4), pp. 91–106.

Stedman, J. (2002) 'Introduction'. In Stedman, J., D. Rothchild and E. Cousens (eds), *Ending Civil Wars: The Implementation of Peace Agreements*. Boulder/London: International Peace Academy and the Centre for International Security and Cooperation: Lynne Rienner, pp. 1–42.

Stedman, J., D. Rothchild and E. Cousens (eds), (2002) *Ending Civil Wars: The Implementation of Peace Agreements*. Boulder/London: International Peace Academy and the Centre for International Security and Cooperation: Lynne Rienner.

The Courier (2003) 'Post-conflict Rehabilitation', No. 198, May–June 2003.

Tull, D. and A. Mehler (2005) 'The Hidden Costs of Power-Sharing: Reproducing Insurgent Violence in Africa', *African Affairs*, 104/416, pp. 375–98.

Ugo, P. 1947. *Introduction to Post-war Reconstruction Programme*. Rome: International Institute of Agriculture.

United Nations (20 Dec 2005) UN Security Council Resolution 1645, S/RES/1645 (2005), http://daccessdds.un.org/doc/UNDOC/GEN/N05/654/17/PDF/N0565417.pdf?OpenElement.

United Nations (1997) Supplement to An Agenda for Peace, A/RES/51/242, 15 September 1997, http://www.un.org/documents/ga/res/51/a51r242.htm.

United Nations (1995) A Supplement to the Agenda for Peace, A/50/60-S/1995/1, 03 January 1995, http://www.un.org/Docs/SG/agsupp.html.

United Nations (1992) An Agenda for Peace, A/47/277-S/24111, 17 June 1992, http://www.un.org/Docs/SG/agpeace.html.

Wentges, J. (1998) 'Force, Function and Phase: Three Dimensions of UN Peacekeeping', *International Peacekeeping*, Vol. 5, No. 3, pp. 58–77.

Whiteman, K. and D. Yates (2004) 'France, Britain, and the United States'. In Adebajo, A. and Ismail, R. (eds), *West Africa's Security Challenges. Building Peace in a Troubled Region*. Boulder and London: Lynne Rienner, pp. 349–82.

Williams, A. (2005) 'Reconstruction' before the Marshall Plan', *Review of International Studies*, 31, pp. 541–58.

Williams, G. (2005) *Engineering Peace: The Military Role in Post-conflict Reconstruction*. Washington: USIP.

Williams, P. (2004) 'Peace Operations and the International Financial Institutions: Insights from Rwanda and Sierra Leone', *International Peacekeeping*, 11(1), pp. 103–23.

Williams, R. (2000) 'Africa and the Challenges of Security Sector Reform'. In Cilliers, J. and A. Hilding-Norberg (eds), *Building Stability in Africa: Challenges for the new millennium*. ISS Monograph 46. Pretoria: Institute for Security Studies.

Woodhouse, T. and O. Ramsbotham (2005) 'Cosmopolitan Peacekeeping and the Globalization of Security', *International Peacekeeping*, Vol. 12, No. 2, pp. 139–56.

World Bank (August 1998) *Conflict Prevention and Post-Conflict Reconstruction: Perspectives and Prospects*. Paris: World Bank Post-Conflict Unit.

Yannis, A. (2003) 'State Collapse and its Implications for Peace Building and Reconstruction'. In Milliken, J. (ed.), *State Failure, Collapse and Reconstruction*. Oxford: Blackwell, pp. 63–82.

Young, C. (2004) 'The End of the Post-Colonial State in Africa? Reflections on Changing African Political Dynamics', *African Affairs*, 103, pp. 23–49.

Youngs, R. (2004) 'Democratic Institution-Building and Conflict Resolution: Emerging EU Approaches', *International Peacekeeping*, Vol. 11, No. 3, pp. 536–43.

Zanotti, L. (2006) 'Taming Chaos: A Foucauldian View of UN Peacekeeping, Democracy and Normalization', *International Peacekeeping*, 13(2), pp. 150–67.

Zartman, I. (1995) 'Posing the Problem of State Collapse'. In Zartman. I. (ed.), *Collapsed States: The Disintegration and Restoration of Legitimate Authority*. Boulder: Lynne Rienner, pp. 1–14.

DISCUSSION PAPERS PUBLISHED BY THE INSTITUTE

Recent issues in the series are available electronically for download free of charge
www.nai.uu.se

1. Kenneth Hermele and Bertil Odén, *Sanctions and Dilemmas. Some Implications of Economic Sanctions against South Africa.* 1988. 43 pp.
SEK 100,- ISBN 91-7106-286-6
2. Elling Njål Tjönneland, *Pax Pretoriana. The Fall of Apartheid and the Politics of Regional Destabilisation.* 1989. 31 pp.
ISBN 91-7106-292-0 (out of print)
3. Hans Gustafsson, Bertil Odén and Andreas Tegen, *South African Minerals. An Analysis of Western Dependence.* 1990. 47 pp.
ISBN 91-7106-307-2 (out of print)
4. Bertil Egerö, *South African Bantustans. From Dumping Grounds to Battlefronts.* 1991. 46 pp.
SEK 100,-. ISBN 91-7106-315-3
5. Carlos Lopes, *Enough is Enough! For an Alternative Diagnosis of the African Crisis.* 1994. 38 pp.
SEK 80,-. ISBN 91-7106-347-1
6. Annika Dahlberg, *Contesting Views and Changing Paradigms.* 1994. 59 pp.
SEK 100,-. ISBN 91-7106-357-9,
7. Bertil Odén, *Southern African Futures. Critical Factors for Regional Development in Southern Africa.* 1996. 35 pp.
ISBN 91-7106-392-7 (out of print)
8. Colin Leys and Mahmood Mamdani, *Crisis and Reconstruction – African Perspectives.* 1997. 26 pp.
SEK 100,-. ISBN 91-7106-417-6
9. Gudrun Dahl, *Responsibility and Partnership in Swedish Aid Discourse.* 2001. 30 pp.
SEK 100,-. ISBN 91-7106-473-7
10. Henning Melber and Christopher Saunders, *Transition in Southern Africa – Comparative Aspects.* 2001. 28 pp.
SEK 100,-. ISBN 91-7106-480-X
11. *Regionalism and Regional Integration in Africa.* 2001. 74 pp. SEK 100,-.
ISBN 91-7106-484-2
12. Souleymane Bachir Diagne, et al., *Identity and Beyond: Rethinking Africanity.* 2001. 33 pp.
SEK 90,-. ISBN 91-7106-487-7
13. Georges Nzongola-Ntalaja, et al., *Africa in the New Millennium.* Edited by Raymond Suttner. 2001. 53 pp.
SEK 90,-. ISBN 91-7106-488-5
14. *Zimbabwe's Presidential Elections 2002.* Edited by Henning Melber. 2002. 88 pp.
ISBN 91-7106-490-7 (out of print)
15. Birgit Brock-Utne, *Language, Education and Democracy in Africa.* 2002. 47 pp.
ISBN 91-7106-491-5 (out of print)
16. Henning Melber et al., *The New Partnership for Africa's development (NEPAD).* 2002. 36 pp.
SEK 90,-. ISBN 91-7106-492-3
17. Juma Okuku, *Ethnicity, State Power and the Democratisation Process in Uganda.* 2002. 42 pp.
SEK 90,-. ISBN 91-7106-493-1
18. Yul Derek Davids, et al., *Measuring Democracy and Human Rights in Southern Africa.* Compiled by Henning Melber. 2002. 50 pp.
SEK 90,-.ISBN 91-7106-497-4
19. Michael Neocosmos, Raymond Suttner and Ian Taylor, *Political Cultures in Democratic South Africa.* Compiled by Henning Melber. 2002. 52 pp.
SEK 110,-. ISBN 91-7106-498-2
20. Martin Legassick, *Armed Struggle and Democracy. The Case of South Africa.* 2002. 53 pp.
SEK 110,. ISBN 91-7106-504-0
21. Reinhart Kössler, Henning Melber and Per Strand, *Development from Below. A Namibian Case Study.* 2003. 32 pp.
ISBN 91-7106-507-5 (out of print)
22. Fred Hendricks, *Fault-Lines in South African Democracy. Continuing Crises of Inequality and Injustice.* 2003. 32 pp.
ISBN 91-7106-508-3 (out of print)
23. Kenneth Good, *Bushmen and Diamonds. (Un) Civil Society in Botswana.* 2003. 39 pp.
SEK 90,-. ISBN 91-7106-520-2 (out of print)
24. Robert Kappel, Andreas Mehler, Henning Melber and Anders Danielson, *Structural Stability in an African Context.* 2003. 55 pp.
ISBN 91-7106-521-0 (out of print)
25. Patrick Bond, *South Africa and Global Apartheid. Continental and International Policies and Politics.* 2004. 45 pp.
ISBN 91-7106-523-7 (out of print)
26. Bonnie Campbell (ed.), *Regulating Mining in Africa. For whose benefit?* 2004. 89 pp.
SEK 110,-.ISBN 91-7106-527-X

27. Suzanne Dansereau and Mario Zamponi, *Zimbabwe – The Political Economy of Decline.* Compiled by Henning Melber. 2005. 43 pp. SEK 90,-. ISBN 91-7106-541-5

28. Lars Buur and Helene Maria Kyed, *State Recognition of Traditional Authority in Mozambique. The nexus of Community Representation and State Assistance.* 2005. 30 pp. SEK 90,-. ISBN 91-7106-547-4

29. Hans Eriksson and Björn Hagströmer, *Chad – Towards Democratisation or Petro-Dictatorship?* 2005. 82 pp. SEK 110,-. ISBN 91-7106-549-0

30. Mai Palmberg and Ranka Primorac (eds), *Skinning the Skunk – Facing Zimbabwean Futures.* 2005. 40 pp. SEK 90,-. ISBN 91-7106-552-0

31. Michael Brüntrup, Henning Melber and Ian Taylor, *Africa, Regional Cooperation and the World Market – Socio-Economic Strategies in Times of Global Trade Regimes.* Compiled by Henning Melber. 2006. 70 pp. SEK 110,-. ISBN 91-7106-559-8

32. Fibian Kavulani Lukalo, *Extended Handshake or Wrestling Match? – Youth and Urban Culture Celebrating Politics in Kenya.* 2006. 58 pp. SEK 110:-. ISBN 91-7106-567-9

33. Tekeste Negash, *Education in Ethiopia: From Crisis to the Brink of Collapse.* 2006. 55 pp. SEK 110,-. ISBN 91-7106-576-8

34. Fredrik Söderbaum and Ian Taylor (eds) *Micro-Regionalism in West Africa. Evidence from Two Case Studies.* 2006. 32 pp. SEK 90,-. ISBN 91-7106-584-9

35. Henning Melber (ed.), *On Africa – Scholars and African Studies.* 2006. 68 pp. SEK 110,-. ISBN 978-91-7106-585-8

36. Amadu Sesay, *Does One Size Fit All? The Sierra Leone Truth and Reconciliation Commission Revisited.* 2007. 56 pp. SEK 110,-. ISBN 978-91-7106-586-5

37. Karolina Hulterström, Amin Y. Kamete and Henning Melber, *Political Opposition in Africn Countries – The Case of Kenya, Namibia, Zambia and Zimbabwe.* 2007. 86 pp. SEK 110,-. ISBN 978-7106-587-2

38. Henning Melber (ed.), *Governance and State Delivery in Southern Africa. Examples from Botswana, Namibia and Zimbabwe.* 2007. 65 pp. SEK 110,-. ISBN 978-91-7106-587-2

39. Cyril Obi (ed.), *Perspectives on Côte d'Ivoire: Between Political Breakdown and Post-Conflict Peace.* 2007. 66 pp. SEK 110,-. ISBN 978-91-7106-606-6

40. Anna Chitando, *Imagining a Peaceful Society. A Vision of Children's Literature in a Post-Conflict Zimbabwe.* 2008. 26 pp. ISBN 978-91-7106-623-7

41. Olawale Ismail, *The Dynamics of Post-Conflict Reconstruction and Peace Building in West Africa. Between Change and Stability.* 2009. 52 pp. ISBN 978-91-7106-637-4

www.ingramcontent.com/pod-product-compliance
Ingram Content Group UK Ltd.
Pitfield, Milton Keynes, MK11 3LW, UK
UKHW051252180426
11947UKWH00020B/1668